Modern Middle East Nations
AND THEIR STRATEGIC PLACE IN THE WORLD

UNITED ARAB EMIRATES

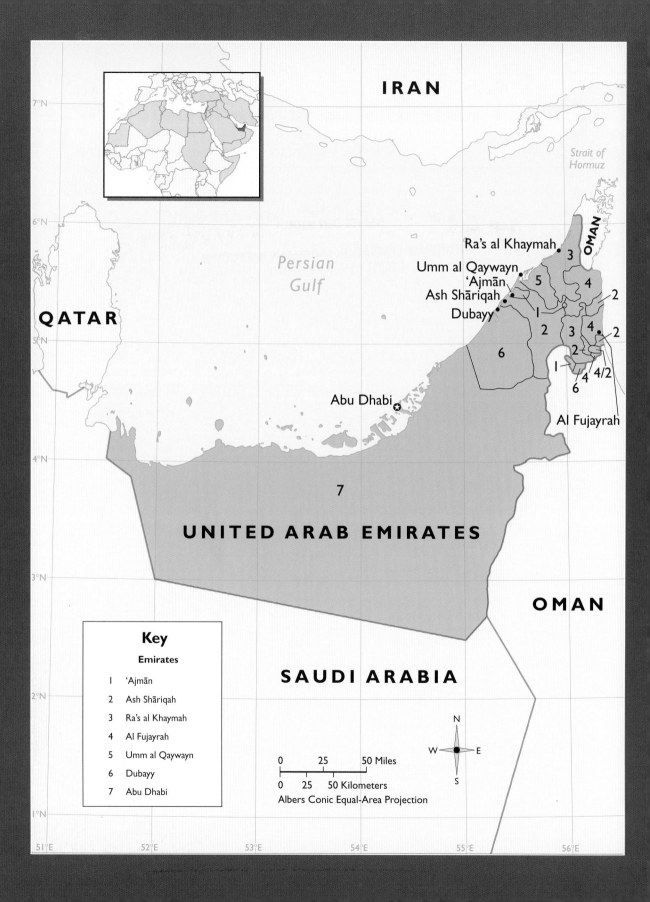

IRAN

Strait of
Hormuz

Persian
Gulf

OMAN

Ra's al Khaymah
●3

Umm al Qaywayn
'Ajmān
Ash Shāriqah
Dubayy

5

4

2

1

2

3

4

2

2

1

4 4/2

6

Al Fujayrah

QATAR

6

Abu Dhabi
★

7

UNITED ARAB EMIRATES

OMAN

SAUDI ARABIA

0   25   50 Miles

0   25   50 Kilometers

Albers Conic Equal-Area Projection

N
W ●E
S

Modern Middle East Nations
AND THEIR STRATEGIC PLACE IN THE WORLD

UNITED ARAB EMIRATES

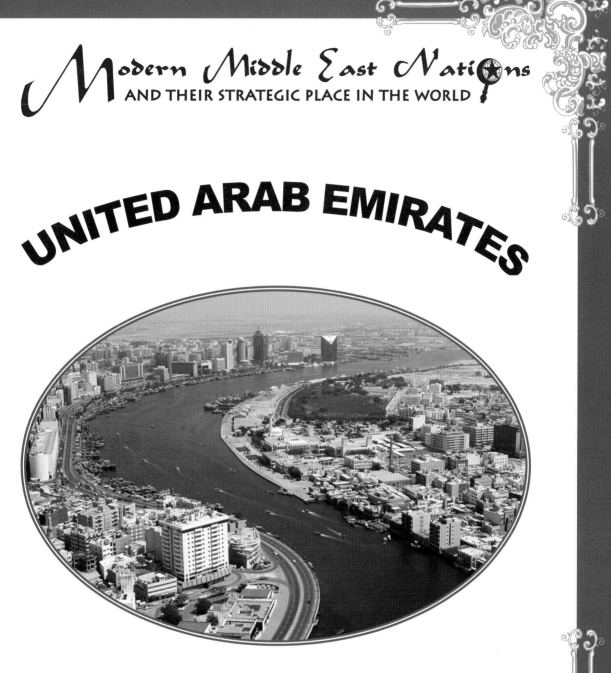

LISA McCOY

MASON CREST PUBLISHERS
PHILADELPHIA

Produced by OTTN Publishing, Stockton, New Jersey

Mason Crest Publishers
370 Reed Road
Broomall, PA 19008
www.masoncrest.com

3 5 7 9 8 6 4

Library of Congress Cataloging-in-Publication Data

McCoy, Lisa.
   United Arab Emirates / Lisa McCoy.
      p. cm. — (Modern Middle East nations and their
strategic place in the world)
Summary: Discusses the geography, history, economy, government,
religion, people, foreign relations, and major cities of the United Arab Emirates.
Includes bibliographical references and index.
   ISBN 1-59084-514-5
1. United Arab Emirates—Juvenile literature.   [1. United Arab Emirates.]
I. Title. II. Series.
DS247.T8M39 2003 953.57—dc21
                                                    2002013013

TABLE OF CONTENTS

Modern Middle East Nations
AND THEIR STRATEGIC PLACE IN THE WORLD

ALGERIA
BAHRAIN
DJIBOUTI
EGYPT
IRAN
IRAQ
ISRAEL
JORDAN
KUWAIT
LEBANON
LIBYA
MAURITANIA
MOROCCO
OMAN
THE PALESTINIANS
QATAR
SAUDI ARABIA
SOMALIA
SUDAN
SYRIA
TUNISIA
TURKEY
UNITED ARAB EMIRATES
YEMEN
THE MIDDLE EAST: FACTS AND FIGURES

Dr. Harvey Sicherman, president and director of the Foreign Policy Research Institute, is the author of such books as *America the Vulnerable: Our Military Problems and How to Fix Them* (2002) and *Palestinian Autonomy, Self-Government and Peace* (1993).

Introduction

by Dr. Harvey Sicherman

Situated as it is between Africa, Europe, and the Far East, the Middle East has played a unique role in world history. Often described as the birthplace of religions (notably Judaism, Christianity, and Islam) and the cradle of civilizations (Egypt, Mesopotamia, Persia), this region and its peoples have given humanity some of its most precious possessions. At the same time, the Middle East has had more than its share of conflicts. The area is strewn with the ruins of fortifications and the cemeteries of combatants, not to speak of modern arsenals for war.

Today, more than ever, Americans are aware that events in the Middle East can affect our security and prosperity. The United States has a considerable military, political, and economic presence throughout much of the region. Developments there regularly find their way onto the front pages of our newspapers and the screens of our television sets.

Still, it is fair to say that most Middle Eastern countries remain a mystery, their cultures and religions barely known, their peoples and politics confusing and strange. The purpose of this book series is to change that, to educate the reader in the basic facts about the 23 states and many peoples that make up the region. (For our purpose, the Middle East also includes the North African states linked by ethnicity, language, and religion to the Arabs, as well as Somalia and Mauritania, which are African but share the Muslim religion and are members of the Arab League.) A notable feature of the series is the integration of geography, demography, and history; economics and politics; culture and religion. The careful student will learn much that he or she needs to know about ever so important lands.

A few general observations are in order as an introduction to the subject matter.

The first has to do with history and politics. The modern Middle East is full of ancient sites and peoples who trace their lineage and literature to antiquity. Many commentators also attribute the Middle East's political conflicts to grievances and rivalries from the distant past. While history is often invoked, the truth is that the modern Middle East political system dates only from the 1920s and was largely created by the British and the French, the victors of World War I. Such states as Algeria, Iraq, Israel, Jordan, Kuwait, Saudi Arabia, Syria, Turkey, and the United Arab Emirates did not exist before 1914—they became independent between 1920 and 1971. Others, such as Egypt and Iran, were dominated by outside powers until well after World War II. Before 1914, most of the region's states were either controlled by the Turkish-run Ottoman Empire or owed allegiance to the Ottoman sultan. (The sultan was also the caliph or highest religious authority in Islam, in the line of the prophet Muhammad's successors, according to the beliefs of the majority of Muslims known as the Sunni.) It was this imperial Muslim system that was ended by the largely British military victory over the Ottomans in World War I. Few of the leaders who emerged in the wake of this event were happy with the territories they were assigned or the borders, which were often drawn by Europeans. Yet, the system has endured despite many efforts to change it.

The second observation has to do with economics, demography, and natural resources. The Middle Eastern peoples live in a region of often dramatic geographical contrasts: vast parched deserts and high mountains, some with year-round snow; stone-hard volcanic rifts and lush semi-tropical valleys; extremely dry and extremely wet conditions, sometimes separated by only a few miles; large permanent rivers and *wadis*, riverbeds dry as a bone until winter rains send torrents of flood from the mountains to the sea. In ancient times, a very skilled agriculture made the Middle East the breadbasket of the Roman Empire, and its trade carried luxury fabrics, foods, and spices both East and West.

Most recently, however, the Middle East has become more known for a single commodity—oil, which is unevenly distributed and largely concentrated in the Persian Gulf and Arabian Peninsula (although large pockets are also to be found in Algeria, Libya, and other sites). There are also new, potentially lucrative offshore gas fields in the Eastern Mediterranean.

This uneven distribution of wealth has been compounded by demographics. Birth rates are very high, but the countries with the most oil are often lightly populated. Over the last decade, Middle East populations under the age of 20 have grown enormously. How will these young people be educated? Where will they work? The failure of most governments in the region to give their people skills and jobs (with notable exceptions such as Israel) has also contributed to large out-migrations. Many have gone to Europe; many others work in other Middle Eastern countries, supporting their families from afar.

Another unsettling situation is the heavy pressure both people and industry have put on vital resources. Chronic water shortages plague the region. Air quality, public sanitation, and health services in the big cities are also seriously overburdened. There are solutions to these problems, but they require a cooperative approach that is sorely lacking.

A third important observation is the role of religion in the Middle East. Americans, who take separation of church and state for granted, should know that most countries in the region either proclaim their countries to be Muslim or allow a very large role for that religion in public life. Among those with predominantly Muslim populations, Turkey alone describes itself as secular and prohibits avowedly religious parties in the political system. Lebanon was a Christian-dominated state, and Israel continues to be a Jewish state. While both strongly emphasize secular politics, religion plays an enormous role in culture, daily life, and legislation. It is also important to recall that Islamic law (*Sharia*) permits people to practice Judaism and Christianity in Muslim states but only as *Dhimmi*, protected but very second-class citizens.

Fourth, the American student of the modern Middle East will be impressed by the varieties of one-man, centralized rule, very unlike the workings of Western democracies. There are monarchies, some with traditional methods of consultation for tribal elders and even ordinary citizens, in Saudi Arabia and many Gulf States; kings with limited but still important parliaments (such as in Jordan and

Morocco); and military and civilian dictatorships, some (such as Syria) even operating on the hereditary principle (Hafez al Assad's son Bashar succeeded him). Turkey is a practicing democracy, although a special role is given to the military that limits what any government can do. Israel operates the freest democracy, albeit constricted by emergency regulations (such as military censorship) due to the Arab-Israeli conflict.

In conclusion, the MODERN MIDDLE EAST NATIONS series will engage imagination and interest simply because it covers an area of such great importance to the United States. Americans may be relative latecomers to the affairs of this region, but our involvement there will endure. We at the Foreign Policy Research Institute hope that these books will kindle a lifelong interest in the fascinating and significant Middle East.

Modern skyscrapers rise behind a venerable mosque in Abu Dhabi, United Arab Emirates. Seven small kingdoms on the coast of the Arabian Peninsula came together to establish the federation in the early 1970s. Today, the UAE is one of the more liberal of the Arab states.

Place in the World

The United Arab Emirates is a land of surprise embodied in vivid contrasts: beautiful coastal areas and desolate inland deserts, high-rise office buildings and Bedouin markets, oil tycoons and turbaned fisherman, great wealth and desert tribes, sports cars and camel racing, and a relaxed lifestyle amid turmoil in the Middle East. This land has much to offer residents, visitors, and the world at large. Although it is one of the youngest nations, its voice is one of power and influence.

The United Arab Emirates (UAE) is a **federation** of seven emirates. Emir is a name for a ruler in Asia or Africa, and an emirate refers to an area that is under the authority of a ruler. The rulers of Abu Dhabi, Dubai, Sharjah, Ajman, Umm al-Qaiwain, and al-Fujairah established this federation on December 2, 1971, for mutual protection and other benefits, but each emirate retains its own identity. The emirate of Ras al-Khaimah joined the federation early in 1972. Six of the emirates are located on the Arabian Peninsula along the southern coast of the Arabian Gulf (also called the Persian Gulf) between the Musandam Peninsula on the east and the Qatar Peninsula on the west. The seventh emirate, al-Fujairah, is located on the north-western coast of the Gulf of Oman, and the emirate of Sharjah also has territory on the Gulf of Oman. Since it was formed, the United Arab Emirates has been under the continuing leadership of Sheikh Zayid bin Sultan al-Nahyan, who rules the federation from the city of Abu Dhabi.

The UAE is one of the more liberal Arab societies in the Middle East, at least with regard to the freedoms permitted to foreigners. Although Islam is the official religion, women from foreign countries are not forced to wear restrictive clothing or adhere closely to Islamic law. However, codes of behavior and dress are far more con-servative in the UAE than in Western nations like the United States. This area, located at the convergence of Asia, Africa, and Europe, has been important for trading purposes for centuries. This land lies near the birthplace of Islam, one of the major religions of the world and one that plays an ever-growing role in world politics.

> **Although the body of water between the Arabian Peninsula and Asia is often called the Persian Gulf, people in the Arab world prefer to call it the Arabian Gulf, as seven of the eight countries that border this important strategic waterway are Arab.**

Although the United Arab Emirates controls an area that is only 32,000 square miles (82,880 square kilometers)—roughly the size of the state of Maine—the UAE is of immense importance both to other coun-tries in the Middle East and to the entire world. This is due to several things. Most important-ly, perhaps, is the fact that the UAE controls massive oil and natural gas reserves. Western countries like the United States depend to a large degree on the oil and natural gas exported by the United Arab Emirates and other countries in the region.

Another reason for the federation's importance is its strategic location on the Arabian Gulf along the approach to the narrow Strait of Hormuz. Around 40 percent of the world's oil travels through the Arabian Gulf. The United States and its allies consider the security of the Gulf States, and of the 500 or so ships that are traveling through the Gulf at any given time, to be of critical concern.

Finally, the emirates have the potential to influence their less-liberal neighbors. While the United Arab Emirates is far from being a democracy in the Western sense of the term, Sheikh Zayid and other leaders place great value on discussion and consensus in the decision-making process.

The UAE is a member of the Arab League, the Organization of Petroleum Exporting Countries (OPEC), the United Nations, and the World Bank. As a member of the Gulf Cooperation Council (GCC), the UAE participates in the structuring of policies having to do with trade, investment banking, defense, and other matters of regional and global concern. The United States, Russia, and the People's Republic of China are just three of the more than 143 countries that have established relations with the UAE. An ambassador of the United States has been in residence in the UAE since 1974.

Just a few short decades ago, the United Arab Emirates was a poor land, but now it is among the wealthiest nations in the world. It is a land filled with people to whom sharing is an important religious commitment and a way of life. Perhaps most importantly, it is a land of careful thought and restraint located near countries with tumultuous and unpredictable rulers.

Thorn trees in the desert, Dubai. More than two-thirds of the UAE's land area is covered by sandy or rocky desert.

The Land

The crescent-shaped UAE is approximately 300 miles (483 kilometers) across at its widest points from east to west and extends 260 miles (418 km) from north to south. Its coastline along the Gulf of Oman and the Arabian Gulf measures 819 miles (1,318 km).

Except for the Hajar Mountains in al-Fujairah, the land is flat, with more than 90 percent of the UAE lying less than 1,000 feet (305 meters) above sea level. Tidal salt flats cover the majority of the coastal area, and the rest of the land is composed mostly of barren desert sands. From the Al Hajar al-Gharbi mountain range, which is located in the northeastern part of the UAE, the land slopes down to an elevated desert plateau and then continues in a gentler slope toward the north coast and west to the Sabkhat Matti. The Sabkhat Matti is a very large salt flat that extends into Saudi Arabia, the UAE's large and influential neighbor to the west. Rainfall that runs off of the mountains sustains a limited amount of natural vegetation on some sections of the plateau.

Four distinct geographical regions characterize the UAE. The largest of these regions by far is the desert interior, as it covers almost 70 percent of the landmass. The next largest area is the region encompassed by the coastal lowlands. The Hajar Mountains make up the third region, and the fourth is composed of over 100 islands scattered off the coast.

REGIONAL TOPOGRAPHY

Desert sands and gravel cover much of the Middle East. Among the most awe-inspiring features of the desert that makes up the interior of the UAE are the impressive sand dunes carved by winds blowing from the northwest toward the southeast over much of the region. Sand is pushed and molded by nature into large dunes, which are said to resemble beautiful, undulating ocean waves. These dunes attain their maximum height in the southeastern part of the UAE where they sometimes extend more that 330 feet (100 meters) above the desert surface! Brutal sandstorms occur often in this area and, for the most part, the inhospitable region remains uninhabited.

An oasis is an area that is green and fertile despite the fact that it is located in an arid region. No natural lakes or rivers lie within the UAE, but there are some underground water deposits. When this precious resource comes to the surface naturally or is brought to the surface by man, an oasis is formed. These areas offer relief and refuge to desert travelers. This is the case with the Liwa Oasis and Buraimi Oasis in the UAE. Wells were dug to tap into the natural ***aquifer***, which is composed of underground layers of stone and dirt that hold water. The water was then brought to the desert surface for human use. Because water is such a valuable commodity in this arid land, wastewater is reprocessed for irrigation.

Most of the United Arab Emirates is low-lying desert land, although the Hajar Mountains run across the eastern part of the country.

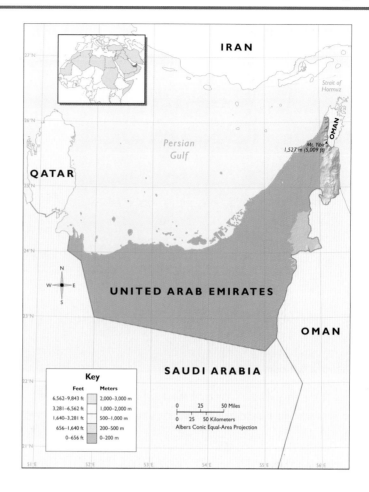

Water is of immense importance in each of the geographical regions of the UAE. When seawater evaporates into the air very quickly, a layer of salt is left behind. This is what takes place along the coast. As a result of this activity, the coastal lowlands are covered with both fine sand and salt flats. The high concentration of salt makes it very difficult for plants and animals to survive in the area. In fact, the only plant life able to thrive in this unwelcoming environment have been a few types of algae.

Yet many lagoons, coves, and **estuaries** are located along the shoreline of the coastal lowlands. Mangrove trees make their home in areas where fresh water and salt water come together. Few land-based plants can survive in this environment, yet this particular

A view of the waterfront of Abu Dhabi. The emirate's position along the coast made it important even before the discovery of oil beneath its sands.

species of tree is noted for its ability not only to survive but also to actually thrive in salty or brackish water. The mangrove trees provide a significant home for shrimp, fish, and birds. Some very impressive mangrove forests are located here, and their preservation is very important to the ecosystem. Conservation of the mangroves has become a priority in the UAE, and a huge effort has been made to save these important trees.

Just like mountains in other parts of the world, the Hajar Mountain range was born under the water during prehistoric times. The ridge that was to become this mountain range began to move upward about 15 to 20 million years ago. Activity caused by **plate tectonics** pushed the ocean floor toward the surface in the eastern part of the Arabian Peninsula. A majestic group of mountains, approximately 20 miles wide and 50 miles from its northernmost to its southernmost peaks, was the result. During the ages that followed, erosion caused by rainwater runoff from higher elevations chiseled deep crevices, known as *wadis*, into the mountainsides. Other than the oases, these landforms are among the few areas that can now sustain vegetation for most of the year. They are, therefore, of great importance to inhabitants of the UAE. Countless residents depend upon these areas for food, and many acres of vegetable plots are made possible in mountain valleys because of water running down from higher elevations.

Of the more than 100 islands included in the UAE, the most significant in terms of size, population, economics, and other factors, is Abu Dhabi. In fact, it is the location of the capital city of the

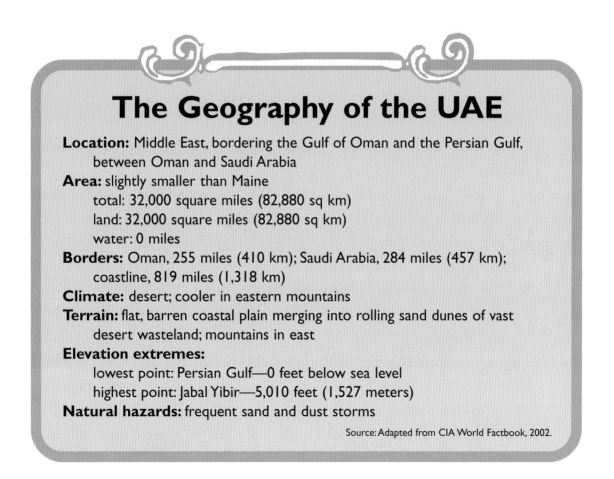

The Geography of the UAE

Location: Middle East, bordering the Gulf of Oman and the Persian Gulf, between Oman and Saudi Arabia

Area: slightly smaller than Maine
    total: 32,000 square miles (82,880 sq km)
    land: 32,000 square miles (82,880 sq km)
    water: 0 miles

Borders: Oman, 255 miles (410 km); Saudi Arabia, 284 miles (457 km); coastline, 819 miles (1,318 km)

Climate: desert; cooler in eastern mountains

Terrain: flat, barren coastal plain merging into rolling sand dunes of vast desert wasteland; mountains in east

Elevation extremes:
    lowest point: Persian Gulf—0 feet below sea level
    highest point: Jabal Yibir—5,010 feet (1,527 meters)

Natural hazards: frequent sand and dust storms

Source: Adapted from CIA World Factbook, 2002.

federation, which is also called Abu Dhabi. Other islands are important to the oil and gas industries because they are utilized as collection points for the resources being obtained from offshore wells. They include Al Mubarraz, Arzanah, Das, and Zirku. The significance of Sir Bani Yas Island lies in the fact that it is the site of an internationally recognized wildlife sanctuary.

CLIMATE

For the most part, the climate of the United Arab Emirates is hot and dry. Severe weather can and does occur during the long summer (May to October). During this time temperatures in the interior can reach 120° Fahrenheit (49° Celsius). Temperatures in the coastal areas usually do not reach quite this level, but along the coast the heat is combined with high humidity, and this can be very uncomfortable. The temperature is usually much more pleasant during the remaining months of the year, when it generally ranges between 68°F and 95°F (20°C and 35°C). Winter weather is sometimes quite windy, but it is usually pleasant across the entire area. Really cold weather is quite rare, although night temperatures in the inland desert can fall to 50°F (10°C).

Annual rainfall is always low but does vary across the land from 1.7 inches (4.3 centimeters) to 5.1 inches (13 cm). It may be surprising, but the UAE can get most of its annual rainfall in one day! This is typical of many of the countries located in the Middle East. Streets that are rarely exposed to water quickly become flooded during a heavy rainfall.

Sandstorms are more common than rainstorms, as they occur with relative frequency. They are often caused by the powerful *shammal*, a strong wind that blows from the north or from the west. The *khamsin*, a hot summer wind that blows from the south, can also trigger sandstorms that sweep across the desert and make it hard to see.

PLANT AND ANIMAL LIFE

Although desert covers most of the United Arab Emirates, it is not devoid of flora and fauna. In fact, the desert offers a unique and even critical habitat for the creatures of this land. Drought-resistant plants (called xerophytes) and salt-tolerant plants (called halophytes) thrive in the environment. Conservation is a priority, and one of the most globally respected sanctuaries for wildlife has been established in the federation.

The most common creatures in the UAE are reptiles. Monitor lizards, spiny-tailed lizards, and geckos are among several species inhabiting this area. Desert snakes prey upon the smaller lizards and also upon rodents and insects. The saw-scaled viper, sand viper, and sand boa all thrive in the desert.

It is more difficult to find plant and animal life in the mountains, although ferns, various grasses, and shrubs can be found and provide food and refuge for the animals that do live there. Among the impressive animals that inhabit the mountain areas are the caracal lynx, Arabian leopard, and the rare Arabian tahr, which is similar to a goat in appearance.

The UAE has instituted programs to protect such creatures as the caracal lynx, pictured here, as well as the rare Arabian oryx and other endangered animals.

Bird life is quite diverse in the UAE, and roughly 400 species have been recorded in the country. While most of these birds are migratory, the number of species breeding in the country has been steadily increasing. More than 80 bird varieties now breed within the UAE. Millions of birds use the UAE as a resting spot during their annual migration across the lower part of the Arabian Gulf. As a result of this active and interesting bird behavior, the UAE has become a popular destination for European tourists interested in bird-watching.

A COMMITMENT TO CONSERVATION

Early in his reign, Sheikh Zayid realized the importance of the environment in the United Arab Emirates and decided that efforts needed to be made to preserve the plants and animals native to the area. Protecting the environment of the UAE is expensive, so the government has turned to the oil industry and private groups to pay a large share of this cost.

Soil erosion has been a major target. A forestation project has been launched, with the dual purpose of reducing erosion and protecting crops from damage caused by harsh winds.

In addition, parts of the desert are now fenced, thus preventing natural vegetation from being trampled or consumed by grazing livestock. This program was made possible through the work of the United Arab Emirates University. Programs like this help to raise the level of understanding among citizens regarding the delicate nature and importance of local habitats and the danger posed to them by farm animals.

The planting of gardens and establishment of parks has been a top priority since oil revenues began to pour into the UAE. In effect, this program is altering the environment and creating new habitats for wildlife.

In 1992, the government formed the Federal Environmental

Agency. The job of this agency is to develop legislation concerning the environment and to promote communication and cooperation between cities and various organizations concerning environmental issues.

Conservation efforts have extended to protection of the native animals, and species that once were in danger of becoming extinct are now being preserved. Hunting in Abu Dhabi was banned more than 15 years ago,

Although governmental institutions for the protection of the environment do exist, namely the Federal Environment Agency and Abu Dhabi's Environmental Research and Wildlife Development Agency, the government stresses that conservation is also the responsibility of the people.

and more recently in the other emirates. The ruler of al-Fujairah has made it illegal to hunt lynx, leopards, and other wildcats that inhabit the mountains. The shooting of gazelles is also discouraged, as these creatures have become rare even in the remote areas of the emirate. However, enforcing restrictions on hunting has been a challenge. For the native Bedouin, hunting is part of their cultural traditions. Convincing them that they should no longer engage in these activities is a difficult task.

Still, some of the animals that inhabit the UAE are in greater danger of extinction. Therefore, the government has been involved in the establishment of captive breeding programs. Programs like this are aimed at protecting a breeding population that can later be used to reestablish a species in the wild. The caracal lynx, Arabian oryx (a type of antelope), sand gazelles, and green turtles are all subjects in captive breeding programs. As a result of a program for endangered animals on the island of Sir Bani Yas, survival of the Arabian gazelle and the Arabian oryx is now assured. Careful reintroduction into the wild has begun for both species.

Ships of the Desert

Life in the desert would not have been possible without the camel. Called "ships of the desert" because of the important role they played in transportation and trade for hundreds of years, camels have been vital to the life and traditions of the UAE. First domesticated sometime between 1200 and 300 B.C., the camel revolutionized desert transportation, creating new opportunities for trade. It is easy to understand why Arabs refer to the camel as "the Gift of God." This animal possesses an amazing ability to adapt and thrive in the desert. Easily surviving on thorny desert plants and able to live for two days without water, this beast of burden can travel as far as 100 miles (160 km) while bearing loads as heavy as 1,000 pounds. Although they are no longer necessary for transportation of most goods, camels continue to be held in high regard for the role they have played throughout history. Traditionally, the camel provided tribal people not only with transportation, but also with milk, meat, hides, and wool.

Education is key to enlisting the support of residents for such programs. Trying to explain to a shepherd that he cannot protect his flock by killing a marauding but rare wildcat that is preying upon it is a great challenge. Success requires education and persuasion—backed up with stiff penalties for breaking the law. But cooperation is increasing among the residents of rural areas. As a result, wild animals are becoming more secure in their natural homes.

The creatures that inhabit the coastal waters of the UAE are also being protected. Thanks to the Ministry of Agriculture and Fisheries, it is now illegal to catch sea turtles or to take their eggs. If a fisherman breaks the law, he is forced to pay a fine. Punishments like this encourage compliance with regulations. In addition, in 1995 the government of the UAE established the first marine park in the Gulf region, in order to protect the beautiful coral reefs off the coast of al-Fujairah, which provide a home to many forms of marine life.

The United Arab Emirates has been a member of the Convention on International Trade in Endangered Species of Flora and Fauna (CITES) since 1990. It is also part of the Regional Organization for the Protection of the Marine Environment (ROPME), along with other GCC countries and Iran.

An ancient watchtower looms over an old mosque in al-Fujairah, one of the smaller emirates of the UAE. The history of human settlement in the region that today is the United Arab Emirates can be traced back more than 5,000 years.

History

Human beings have had a rich and varied history in the Middle East for thousands of years. Having been created in 1971, the United Arab Emirates is a young country. Yet the presence of human settlements in this part of the Arabian Peninsula can be traced back to at least 3000 B.C. A group of underground aquifers located beneath this arid land played a role in making it a cultural crossroad.

The period of history dating from about 3500 B.C. to 1500 B.C. is known as the Bronze Age because it was during this time that humans discovered how to create weapons and tools from this alloy of copper and tin. Evidence of Bronze Age settlements existing in the area now known as the United Arab Emirates has been found in the foothills of the Hajar Mountains.

Archaeologists conducting research near Abu Dhabi have recovered more evidence of early man. Here artifacts linked to

This clay vessel from Umm an-Nar dates to around 2500 B.C. Umm an-Nar is an island near present-day Abu Dhabi that was a center for long-distance commerce.

a trading culture that existed in the area in about 3000 B.C. have been discovered. The tombs of members of this society exhibit excellent **masonry** (including detailed carvings of local animal life such as gazelles and camels) and indicate that the civilization was probably quite advanced. The influence of these people probably extended along the coast into the area that today is Oman and into the desert interior. The ruins of ancient cities also point to the advanced nature of this civilization now known as Umm an-Nar.

Water wells located in the centers of fortress towers tell us that the people who lived here were probably successful farmers. These village wells may have been used to irrigate vegetables, grains, and fruits such as date palms. The fact that this cultural group engaged in extensive trading with people living as far away as Egypt, India, Mesopotamia (modern-day Iraq), and Persia (modern-day Iran) is indicated by pottery remains and other artifacts that have been discovered in Al Ain and Ras al-Khaimah as well as Abu Dhabi.

THE BEDOUIN

As might be expected, survival in this harsh desert land was a struggle for the inhabitants. This was not a lush, green land that could support huge groups of people and animals. Survival depended upon obtaining food, and in this environment that meant small-scale farming near oases, which were isolated from each other. People lived in small tribal groups and engaged in **nomadic** grazing of animals, moving their herds to various locations in order to find vegetation to feed them. People living closer to coastal areas or traveling to these areas seasonally engaged in fishing and diving for pearls.

Bedouin is the name usually given to the people living in these nomadic tribal groups. Bedouin women often stayed at more permanent encampments located on the oases while the men herded sheep, goats, and camels from one grazing area to another.

Of the crops utilized by this group of people, none was more versatile and significant than the date palm. No part of this important plant went to waste. Dates provided food for animals as well as

Bedouins lead their camels through the desert, United Arab Emirates.

for people, and the branches and trunks of these trees yielded the building material needed to make houses, boats, and fishing traps. It was also used as fuel for cooking fires. Fibers of the tree were used to make rope, and even the leaves were useful when made into fans, baskets, and floor mats.

For some time, the Bedouin maintained a successful existence in their small trading communities. These nomads established trade routes with people living as far away as China. Eventually, various Persian empires overpowered the Bedouin, gaining control of their maritime trade routes. The Achaemenid Empire ruled the territory from about the sixth to the fourth centuries B.C. From the third to the seventh centuries A.D. the region was under the control of the Sassanid Empire.

Arab tribes began to move into the region in large numbers between about 200 and 600 A.D. They came from the north and along the southern coast. Their arrival preceded the emergence of a unifying new religion—Islam.

THE DEVELOPMENT AND SPREAD OF ISLAM

During the sixth and seventh centuries, some of the most historically significant events for the future of the world were taking place on the Arabian Peninsula. Among them was the birth of the prophet Muhammad in about A.D. 570. This orphan boy grew up under his uncle's guidance to become a businessman. During this time war was common among tribes, as was the worship of many gods. Muhammad chose to worship one god. When he was about 40 years old, Muhammad decided to spend some time in meditation. Muslims (the name given to people who practice the faith of Muhammad) believe that while he was on this retreat and living in a cave in the mountains, the archangel Gabriel visited him and revealed the Word of Allah.

Islam (the name given to the faith begun by Muhammad) began

to emerge in the Saudi Arabian city of Mecca after Muhammad ended his isolation and began reciting the revelations that he had learned from Gabriel. Many people rejected the teachings and ridiculed Muhammad. Eventually Muhammad and his followers moved to the city of Medina, where his teachings were better received. People began to memorize the teachings. Later they would write them down in what became the Qur'an (or Koran), the holy book of Islam. After several years, Muhammad and a group of followers returned to Mecca, where they destroyed idols and took the city by force. At this time many residents of Mecca converted to Muhammad's new faith.

In the year 630, an emissary of the prophet Muhammad arrived

Muhammad receives a message from Allah in this illustration. Around the year 610, Muhammad began to preach a message that there was only one god, Allah, to the polytheistic people of Mecca. His teachings became the basis for a new religion, Islam.

in southeastern Arabia with an invitation to the people of this land to convert to Islam. Like most of the people in other Arab nations, the tribal people of the area that was to become the UAE accepted this invitation.

After Muhammad's death in 632, grave disagreements arose among the followers of Islam over who should take the prophet's place, becoming the new religious leader. Wars erupted between those who desired Islamic rule over Arabia and those who did not. Dibba, which is located along the Gulf of Oman in the present-day emirates of Sharjah and al-Fujairah, was the site of an intense battle. Eventually, the Muslim forces gained victory. The fact that the Muslims were victorious remains a critical factor, influencing all facets of Arabian society even to this day.

Under the **caliphs**, the Arabs conquered many lands. They built huge palaces and other buildings. Their ships sailed on the Mediterranean Sea. Laws were enacted and enforced, taxes were collected, and science was improved. Ancient Greek texts covering topics such as astronomy, physics, medicine, chemistry, mathematics, geography, pharmacology, and philosophy were translated and preserved by Arabian scholars. Some of these texts survived only because of these translations. The Arabs added much to world knowledge of geography. They also introduced Arabic numerals and advanced mathematics, particularly algebra. Along with their accomplishments, the Arabs spread Islam into Asia, Africa, and even western Europe.

The literal translation of the word *Islam* is "submission." The religion teaches followers to believe in one God, who is called Allah, and to submit to His will.

During this time the capital of the Arab world shifted to several successive cities. The center of power eventually moved out of Arabia. Toward the end of the eighth century, the Abbasid dynasty of caliphs moved the capital to Baghdad in Mesopotamia. In the tenth century, a new Muslim sect called the Carmathians took over control of Arabia, but toward the end of that century they lost control to several Bedouin tribes. This meant that Arabia was once again the scene of conflict between several groups, even though between 1075 and 1094 the spiritual leadership of the Abbasid caliph in Baghdad was acknowledged.

The Mongols conquered Baghdad in 1258, and this ended any influence over Arabia by the Abbasids. A class of soldier-slaves who had seized power in Egypt, the Mamluks, gained control of Mecca and some other parts of Arabia in 1269. When the Ottoman Turks successfully conquered the Egyptians in 1517, the Turks gained considerable control over parts of Arabia.

Meanwhile, Europeans had begun to experience a Renaissance of scientific thought. Much of the Renaissance knowledge was based on ancient writings that had been preserved in Arabic centers of learning, such as Andalusia and Córdoba, during the Middle Ages in Europe. The rulers of such European countries as Portugal, Spain, England, and the Netherlands began to send sailors out on voyages to discover unknown lands and open new trade routes.

For the nomadic Bedouin, desert life remained mostly unchanged during this long period of history. Flocks were herded and trading took place with neighboring groups. Trading was especially important to people living in cities near the Strait of Hormuz. They engaged in this activity in the Arabian Gulf and the Indian Ocean. When the Europeans arrived on the scene, this period of relative calm for traders and people living in coastal areas ended.

THE EUROPEAN PRESENCE IN THE GULF

During the late 15th century and early 16th century, Portuguese explorers and traders began to arrive in the Arabian Gulf area.

In 1497–99, Vasco da Gama sailed around the southernmost tip of Africa and into the Indian Ocean, established trade agreements with local rulers, then returned to Portugal. Soon, the king of Portugal sent warships to the region to protect the trade route, and by 1520 the Portuguese controlled important coastal areas of the Arabian Peninsula.

During most of the 15th century the Portuguese had made voyages along the western coast of Africa, charting the routes along the coast of that continent. In 1497–99, the Portuguese explorer Vasco da Gama sailed around the southernmost tip of Africa, then north to the Indian Ocean. There, he negotiated trade agreements with local rulers.

However, the direct trade route established by Portugal meant that Arab merchants were cut out of the lucrative spice trade with Europe. They began to harass Portuguese trading vessels. As a result, Portugal decided to send troops and warships to protect their merchant ships and trading posts. By 1520, Portuguese forces had captured several coastal cities in the area of the United Arab Emirates.

The Portuguese were strict rulers, but they did allow local leaders to remain in control—with certain stipulations. For one thing, the Arab rulers had to pay tribute to the Portuguese in the form of heavy taxes.

The Portuguese maintained control over the area until 1633. During the early 17th century, the shah, or ruler, of Persia (modern-day Iran) decided he no longer wanted to pay the Portuguese taxes. He invited two other European powers, the Netherlands and Great Britain, to come to the Gulf as Persian allies. If they would help Persia eliminate the Portuguese presence, the Persian shah promised the Dutch and the British half of the income generated at Persian ports. Soon the Portuguese were forced to abandon the region.

> Greeks and Romans originally referred to the area of the Arabian Peninsula as the East. When European explorers reached India, Japan, and China in the 15th and 16th centuries, they were reaching lands farther east of the Mediterranean than they had traveled before. That is when the area of the Arabian Peninsula began to be called the Near East and lands farther east were called Far East. After World War I, the term Middle East began to be used.

Although the British and the Dutch had cooperated to rid the area of the Portuguese, they were soon at odds for control of the Arabian Gulf. By the late 17th century, Britain was the dominant power in the area. For the next 300 years, the British would exert a strong influence on the Trucial States (a name given to the small emirates on the coast before they became the United Arab Emirates in the 1970s).

An important religious movement during the 18th century forever changed life on the Arabian Peninsula. During the 1730s, a man named Muhammad ibn Abd al-Wahhab started a religious revival, preaching for stricter adherence to the Islamic laws established by the prophet Muhammad and the caliphs that followed him. These beliefs have become known as Wahhabi Islam, although practitioners refer to themselves as *muwahiddun* (unitarians, or believers in a single god). Those who followed Wahhabi beliefs were also opposed to the presence of Europeans in the Arabian Gulf.

In 1744, Muhammad ibn Abd al-Wahhab made an agreement with Muhammad ibn Saud, the ruler of a small Arabian settlement. They agreed to establish a new state based on the principles of Wahhabi Islam. During the remainder of the 18th century and the 19th century, Muhammad ibn Saud and his family—the Al Saud—battled with the Ottoman Turks, who claimed to rule the Arabian Peninsula, as well as with other Arabs who did not accept the teachings of Muhammad ibn Abd al-Wahhab.

THE HISTORY OF THE TRUCIAL STATES

Many of the Arab tribes that lived along the coast of the Arabian Gulf accepted Wahhabism. One of the strongest of these were the Bani Yas, which decided not to challenge the maritime superiority of the British. Another tribe, the Qawasim, were more fervent in their Wahhabi beliefs, particularly the opposition to Western influences. After the British signed a treaty with the Al Bu Said family, which ruled Oman, the Qawasim began attacking British ships that entered their waters. The British interpreted these attacks as piracy, and began to refer to this area of the Arabian Gulf as "the Pirate Coast."

Because they wanted to protect their trade route with India, the British launched an attack and burned the port of Ras al-Khaimah and other coastal harbors in 1819. In 1820, the determined British fleet claimed a dramatic victory over the Qawasim by systematically capturing or destroying every Qawasim ship that could be located. That was followed by the imposition by Britain of a General Treaty of Peace and the installation of a military post in the region. This was the first of several treaties imposed by the British. Nine Arab sheikhdoms were located in the area covered by the treaty.

Even after the treaty was signed, however, occasional raids against British ships continued until 1835. At that point the sheikhs agreed not to participate in further raids. In 1853 the sheikhs signed the Treaty of Perpetual Peace, agreeing to a lasting maritime truce. The series of treaties with the British is the source of the names "Trucial Sheikhdoms" or "Trucial States" by which this area became known. The Arab sheikhdoms were forced to accept British protection and agreed to obtain permission from the British before dealing with any foreign powers. This protectorate agreement would remain in effect until 1971.

Great Britain remained the major imperial power in this region, even though the Ottoman Empire claimed control over the entire Arabian Peninsula. However, the area of Ottoman control was largely contained to the western part of the peninsula, and fighting between the Wahhabis, led by the Al Saud, and the Turks continued until after World War I.

During the First World War (1914–1918), the British agent T. E. Lawrence (nicknamed "Lawrence of Arabia") urged the Arabs to rise up against the Ottomans, who had sided with Britain's opponents, the Central Powers (Germany and Austria-Hungary). When the war ended with a victory by the Allies (Great Britain, France, and the United States) the once-proud Ottoman Empire collapsed. The victorious Allies divided the former Ottoman provinces into smaller countries, most of which were placed under either British or French control.

Six years of civil war on the Arabian Peninsula followed, during which several chieftains fought for control. In 1932, the kingdom of Saudi Arabia was formed under the leadership of Sultan Abd al-Aziz al-Saud. This kingdom controlled most of the peninsula. However, the Trucial States along the Gulf coast maintained their autonomy under British control. The British presence in the Trucial States provided a measure of stability during the next few decades.

After the Second World War ended in 1945, however, Great Britain could no longer afford to maintain its far-flung colonial empire. In 1947, India gained independence from Great Britain. Because the British had become involved in the Gulf mainly to protect its trade with this important part of the empire, the loss of India reduced Britain's will to maintain a presence in the Arabian Gulf. Instead, they decided to withdraw from the area.

The British decided to remain in the Gulf because of the discovery of oil in the Trucial States during the late 1950s. Oil exports began in 1962. The rulers of the Trucial States were able to use the great amounts of money that they received in return for the oil in

With Great Britain and the Ottoman Empire on opposite sides of World War I, the British sent agent T. E. Lawrence (1888–1935) to the Arabs, hoping he could convince them to rise up against their Ottoman rulers. "Lawrence of Arabia," as he became known, encouraged the Arab Revolt, which helped capture Syria, Palestine, and other territories from the Ottoman forces. However, though Lawrence himself supported the cause of Arab nationalism, after the war control over the Arab lands was split among the victorious powers, Great Britain and France. Little changed in the Trucial States, which maintained their longstanding ties to Britain.

order to begin building roads, hospitals, government buildings, and airports, making life easier for the people living there.

In 1968, Britain announced it would withdraw from the Gulf region by 1971. The local rulers did not want to be independent; they liked being under British protection. Great Britain, how-

When the British outlawed slavery along the Arabian coast, the trade was taken over by the Bani Yas. A major slave market developed in Eastern Arabia, and continued to hold its position into the 1950s.

ever, was determined to leave the area.

The original plan developed by the British was to create one state consisting of Qatar, Bahrain, and the Trucial States. That plan met with almost immediate failure, as the nations involved were not able to agree on how authority would be shared. Bahrain wanted to have a greater share of power than the other areas. When this request was denied, Bahrain declared its independence separately. Qatar soon followed suit.

Merging the remaining emirates into a cohesive political unit was an extremely difficult task. Complex issues needed to be discussed and resolved, and the rulers needed to agree on how to divide authority among the emirates and the federal government. Long-standing tribal traditions of consultation and consensus had been successful for the emirates in the past. The rulers of the emirates recognized the need to incorporate these honored methods of negotiation as they worked out details of the federation and to include them in their future form of government.

The United Arab Emirates gained full independence on December 2, 1971. It consisted at first of six emirates; a seventh, Ras al-Khaimah, joined the federation in 1972. Sheikh Zayid bin Sultan al-Nahyan was elected president of the UAE.

Leaders of the United Arab Emirates celebrate the 25th anniversary of their independence in 1996. The emirates gained full independence from Great Britain on December 2, 1971.

When negotiations led to the establishment of the UAE, many people did not take the new federation seriously. Instead, it was considered a British creation. While it is true that the British masterminded the plan behind the federation, the emirs who ruled the smaller sheikhdoms with fewer resources realized that their territories had little hope of surviving as independent states. Despite the poor opinions many had of the federation at its founding, the UAE has emerged today as one of the most stable governments in the Middle East and has developed into a major center of international business.

It is not just the discoveries of oil and gas that have led to economic prosperity in the area. In the late 1970s, the ruler of the emirate of Dubai had a revolutionary idea to stimulate economic development. He began to develop a business zone that would be free of taxation and completely open to all businesses, even those with 100 percent foreign ownership. The establishment of this "free zone" has brought millions of dollars into the UAE.

Along with economic success the federation has faced many political crises. Immediately after formation of the federation, Iran seized several islands that had been claimed by the United Arab Emirates, including Tunb al Kubrá (Greater Tunb), Tunb al Sughrá (Lesser Tunb), and Abu Musá. Though armed conflict has not taken place, this territorial dispute has yet to be resolved.

There have been several other major threats to regional stability in the area, including the Iranian Islamic Revolution of 1979 and the Iran-Iraq War (1980–1988), which ended in a cease-fire agreement negotiated by the United Nations.

During the invasion of Kuwait by Iraq in 1990 and the subsequent Gulf War (1990–1991), the UAE was a

Iranians pull down a statue of their former ruler, the Reza Shah Pahlavi, after his son, Mohammed Reza Shah Pahlavi, left the country in January 1979. The Iranian Revolution threatened to upset the stability of the Middle East.

friend and ally of the west, cooperating with the United States and other countries during the Gulf War to overpower Iraqi aggression.

The UAE experienced an international financial scandal in 1991, when fraud and forgery charges resulted in the shutdown of the Bank of Credit and Commerce International's (BCCI) global operations. Sheikh Zayid was one of the founding shareholders of the BCCI. Approximately $2 billion was lost to investors and businesses located in Abu Dhabi during this fiscal crisis. In 1993, a civil suit was filed against BCCI and 13 of its leading officers by the government of Abu Dhabi. Interestingly, it was in a U.S. federal court that the former chief executive of the BCCI pled guilty to charges of fraud, conspiracy, and *racketeering*.

The United Arab Emirates have survived every crisis and even prospered during them. Sheikh Zayid deserves much credit for the continuing prosperity and security of the UAE amid the crises that have surrounded them. He has wisely allocated revenues from oil sales in Abu Dhabi to ensure the international security of the entire UAE. The United Arab Emirates has emerged as a strong voice and influential power for moderation in the Middle East.

Sheikh Zayid bin Sultan al-Nahyan, the ruler of Abu Dhabi, has been the president of the United Arab Emirates since the federation was created in 1971.

The United Arab Emirates has made a fascinating transition from one of the poorest nations in the Middle East to one of the richest and most influential. Over the last several decades it has become a member of many international organizations. It is a land of contrasts, maintaining its nomadic desert culture while at the same time developing as a world-class center of banking and business. The tribes in the United Arab Emirates consist of interrelated families, and all native citizens of the UAE have tribal membership. The discovery of oil has brought many changes to the UAE, but among the important things that have remained unchanged are the structure of the family and the intense feelings of tribal solidarity. The proud people of Bedouin descent hold the memories of their fathers and forefathers close to their hearts. Their dignity, strength, and courage are remembered, respected, admired, and preserved.

Tribal Families in the UAE

Each of the seven geographic areas that compose the United Arab Emirates has a ruler and a history of its own. Tribal history is of major importance to this region. This tribal structure, characterized by very strong family ties, was well suited to survival in a desert land where the resources are limited.

The tribal traditions in this part of the Arabian Peninsula probably began in the second century A.D. The part of the Arabian Peninsula that is covered by the Rub al-Khali desert is known as the Empty Quarter. Two major migrations into this area are now thought to have begun in Yemen, which is located in the southernmost part of the Arabian Peninsula. The first group of nomads reached the area of Al Ain, in what is now the UAE, by traveling along the coast of Oman and through the Hajar Mountains. It is believed that the other major group of people traveled via the Nejd (a plateau in central Arabia) and eastern Saudi Arabia. Both of these groups were attracted to the oases located in Al Ain.

Four predominant tribal groups are located in the Abu Dhabi emirate. They are the Manasir, Dhawahir, Awamir, and the Bani Yas. The Bani Yas is further divided into a federation of almost a dozen smaller tribes. These groups have dominated the Liwa Oasis and the towns of Al Ain and Abu Dhabi. The rulers of Abu Dhabi have traditionally come from the Al Bu Falah tribe. In addition to territorial control, each of these tribes specialized in one element of the economy. Pearling (fishing for pearls) played an important role in the lives of the Quibaisat and the Rumaithat, important subgroups of the Bani Yas, until the decline of the industry. Other subgroups of the Bani Yas are the Hawamil, the Mazari, and the Sudan.

The Bani Yas moved into Abu Dhabi in 1793. The tribe became prosperous, and continued to grow during the 19th and 20th centuries. As a result, the Bani Yas were able to dominate both Dubai and Abu Dhabi, becoming the major ruling tribe in the UAE. Sheikh Zayid bin Khalifah Al Bu Falah strengthened the power of the Bani Yas during his reign over Abu Dhabi, which lasted from 1866 to 1909.

The group's power and authority have been less assured and more strained in Dubai, where rivalry exists between the main tribe and the Al Bu Falasah, a subgroup of the Bani Yas. The Al Bu Falasah broke away in 1833 and founded Dubai; the current Al Maktoum rulers of the emirate are descended from this group.

The emirates of Ras al-Khaimah and Sharjah have been dominated by the Qawasim, a clan that emerged in the 18th century as a subgroup of the Huwalah, a powerful tribe. The Qawasim were powerful seafaring warriors who controlled the Strait of Hormuz, and at one time controlled large areas of land on the coast of Persia and in Arabia. The Qawasim were able to rule their territory largely because of their reputation and ability at sea, but they were

An aerial view shows the port at Abu Dhabi as it appears today.

regarded as pirates by the British, who saw control of the Arabian Gulf as critical to their trade with India. This led to decades of fighting during the 19th century.

The Al Sharqiyyin established control of the al-Fujairah emirate, one of the largest in the UAE, and the dynasty that rules today is composed of members of this tribe. Though larger than some of the other emirates, it was 1952 before al-Fujairah was officially recognized as an emirate in its own right.

With the city of Umm al-Qaiwain as their major place of residence, the Al Moalla and Al Ali are the dominant tribes of the Umm al-Quwain emirate. The rulers of the emirate are members of the Al Moalla.

The Al Nuaimi is the ruling tribe in the emirate of Ajman.

The Great Mosque in Al Ain, an oasis town in Abu Dhabi. Most of the people living in the United Arab Emirates practice Islam, a monotheistic religion that dates back nearly 1,400 years.

The Economy, Politics, and Religion

Prior to becoming a federation, the harsh living conditions in the small countries of the UAE offered tribal residents little more than **subsistence**. Although some trading did take place, for the most part people were too busy obtaining food and shelter for their families to produce goods for export. By contrast, today the United Arab Emirates has an annual **gross domestic product** (GDP) of some $50 billion, and its citizens have a standard of living that is as high or higher than many Western nations. The major reason for the strength of the United Arab Emirates' economy lies with the discovery of oil reserves and the development of that industry.

The Importance of Oil and Gas

Before the discovery of oil and gas reserves, diving for pearls was one of the major occupations in the area now known as the United Arab Emirates. Herding, fishing, and agriculture were the other major industries. No formal schools, factories, hospitals, or even paved roads existed in the UAE before oil was discovered in the middle of the 20th century.

In the 1930s, Sheikh Saeed, then the ruler of Dubai, became the first of the emirs to grant the British permission to drill for oil. Shortly thereafter, the sheikh of Abu Dhabi followed suit. However, it was not until 1959 that the first large oil reserve was discovered off the coast of Abu Dhabi. Desert exploration in Abu Dhabi led to the discovery of huge reserves a year later. In Dubai, a large oil field

An oil rig in the harbor of Abu Dhabi. Production of oil and natural gas accounts for more than one-third of the UAE's annual gross domestic product—the total value of all goods and services produced within the federation in a year.

Obaid bin Sail al-Nasseri, the UAE's minister of petroleum and mineral resources, prepares for a meeting of the Organization of Petroleum Exporting Countries (OPEC). Abu Dhabi, which controls more than 90 percent of the UAE's oil, has been a member of OPEC since 1967, although Dubai, with the second-largest reserve of oil among the emirates, has never joined the organization.

was discovered in 1966. Smaller reserves were found in Ras al-Khaimah and Sharjah.

The transition from a subsistence economy to one based on the export of oil took place in an incredibly short period of time. Since oil exports began in 1962, the money received for the UAE's oil has made it possible for tall buildings to rise from the desert and for camel trails to become paved highways.

In 1973, the prices being paid for oil rose substantially. In addition to direct earnings from export, this provided revenue for investments. Today, the Abu Dhabi Investment Authority manages very large investments in the West. These investments are estimated to have a value of approximately $150 billion.

Almost 80 percent of the export earnings of the UAE come from

> Countries in the Arabian Gulf region control more than 60 percent of the world's crude oil reserves and over 35 percent of its natural gas reserves.

oil and gas, yet this segment of the economy accounts for only 34 percent of the gross domestic product (GDP), which stood at $51 billion in 2001. Annual oil production in the UAE amounts to approximately 852 million barrels (more than 2 million barrels per day). It has been predicted that, if current rates of removal are maintained, oil will be available in the UAE for over 150 years and gas for over 200 years. Although this does represent an extended period of time, the UAE's rulers have been wise to realize that there is a limit to these resources and to strive for economic diversity before oil and gas reserves are exhausted.

The UAE is an influential member of the Organization of Petroleum Exporting Countries (OPEC). OPEC's goal is to keep the price of oil profitable for all of its members by controlling oil production. Toward this end, it decides on a quota for each country in its membership. The number of barrels of oil each country can produce is based on the amount of oil reserves within that country. The UAE has supported a moderate oil-pricing policy, which it feels will provide the maximum benefit to the country over the longest period of time. The UAE also has membership in the Organization of Arab Petroleum Exporting Countries (OAPEC). This organization works to coordinate oil policy among Arab nations.

As would be expected, most electricity in the UAE is generated by power plants that burn either oil or gas. Naturally the production of **potable** water is extremely important in an arid land. Technology exists to turn seawater into potable water, but the process uses much energy. In many areas of the world this high-energy use results in a high cost of water desalination, thus prohibiting use of the technology. Abundant petrochemical resources make it possible to utilize the technology in the UAE, however.

MANUFACTURING AND AGRICULTURE

Another reason for the tremendous economic growth within the United Arab Emirates has been the concept and development of an area free of taxation, known as the Jebel Ali Free Zone. Credit for this idea goes to Sheikh Maktoum bin Rashid al-Maktoum of Dubai. Located approximately 30 miles (48 km) from Dubai, the area falls under the supervision of the Jebel Ali Free Zone Authority (JAFZA), which was created in 1985. This area is attractive to investors because it offers 100 percent foreign ownership of businesses

The Economy of the UAE

Gross domestic product (GDP*): $51 billion (2001)
GDP per capita: $21,100 (2001)
Inflation: 4.5%
Natural resources: petroleum, natural gas
Agriculture (3% of GDP): dates, vegetables, watermelons; poultry, eggs, dairy products; fish
Industry (46% of GDP): petroleum, fishing, petrochemicals, construction materials, boat building, handicrafts, pearling
Services (51% of GDP): government, banking, education, tourism, other
Foreign trade:
    Imports—$28.6 billion: machinery and transport equipment, chemicals, food
    Exports—$47.6 billion: crude oil, natural gas, reexports, dried fish, dates
Currency exchange rate: 3.673 Emirati dirhams = $1 U.S. (2003)

*GDP, or gross domestic product, is the total value of goods and services produced in a country annually.
All figures are 2000 estimates unless otherwise noted.
Sources: CIA World Factbook, 2002.

The aircraft carrier USS *Enterprise* enters the port of Mina Jabal Ali, Dubai, one of the world's largest artificial deepwater ports.

without any personal or corporate income taxes, and there are no currency restrictions.

The Jebel Ali complex is home to over 200 factories, including a steel fabrication manufacturer and an aluminum smelter. Reebok, Safeway, Xerox, Sony, Black & Decker, and Honda are among more than 1,500 mulitnational companies that now conduct business in the Jebel Ali Free Zone.

Mina Jabal Ali, located in Dubai near the Jebel Ali Free Zone, is one of the world's largest artificial deepwater ports. It is one of 15 ports that operate in the United Arab Emirates. The fact that a deepwater port and the free-trade zone are located here makes the area extremely attractive for both the manufacture and distribution of goods. This area has become home to an extremely profitable reexport trade, meaning goods are purchased and imported into the country, then sold and exported back out of the country at a profit. Among the countries that goods are reexported to are Iran, Pakistan, India, Kuwait, and Saudi Arabia, along with countries in East Africa. Mina Jabal Ali is supported by a modern transportation system, full electrical capabilities, and communication systems, along with the availability of a well-trained labor force.

Manufacturing of textiles, clothing, chemicals, plastics, paint, building materials, and other products has grown rapidly during recent years. Manufactured products accounted for 19 percent of the GDP in 1996; today they account for more than 25 percent. With the exception of companies located in the free trade zone in Dubai, citizens of the UAE must have 51 percent of the ownership in all businesses operating within the country.

Although agriculture accounts for only 3 percent of the GDP, it is important to the residents of the UAE because the level of self-sufficiency they have achieved means they do not have to depend on imported foods in certain categories. Farmers account for 5 percent of the work force, and dairy products, eggs, alfalfa, tobacco, fruits, and many vegetables are produced locally. Dates have been a staple crop for centuries, and the level of production allows for export as well as domestic use. Although farms are much smaller than those in the United States, they are supported by government **subsidies**, making farming a more attractive and profitable activity. Dairy farming takes place on a fertile plain in Ras al-Khaimah. Crops are grown in the Hajar Mountains of al-Fujairah, around the Buraimi Oasis, and on an island off the coast of Abu Dhabi.

In recent years, the United Arab Emirates has brought in much more money from its exports than it has spent on imports. This, plus the fact that revenue from oil and gas make up less than half the country's export revenue, is evidence of the UAE's successful

Colorful electric signs illuminate the street that runs through a souk in Dubai.

diversification efforts. Among the countries that purchase the UAE's exports are Japan, India, South Korea, Iran, and Oman.

Seventy percent of the goods imported into the country can be classified as machinery, transportation equipment, or other manufactured goods. Major sources for products being imported into the UAE are the United States, the United Kingdom, Japan, Italy, India, and South Korea.

SERVICES, TRANSPORTATION, AND TOURISM

Social services offered by various communities have consistently grown. These include free health care, free housing in rural areas, and subsidized housing in urban areas. Employment opportunities exist for teachers and in government offices. Services, including government operations and real estate among others, account for about half of the GDP today.

As revenues from oil sales became available, development of an efficient transportation system became a top priority for the UAE. Today, the emirates are connected to each other by a series of modern highways, and the automobile is the most commonly utilized form of transportation. Saudi Arabia and Oman are also easily accessible by this system, consisting of approximately 2,538 miles (4,085 km) of paved roads.

Six airports service the UAE; the largest of them is Dubai International Airport. Emirates Airlines is owned by Dubai while Oman, Bahrain, and Abu Dhabi share ownership of Gulf Air.

Tourists from around the world have been attracted to the UAE because of its mild winter weather and extensive beaches. Areas of scenic and historic interest are also popular. Exotic shopping opportunities can be found in the souks (markets), and visitor accommodations are among the most modern and well equipped in the world. As if that weren't enough, the area is well known for duty-free shopping. The combination of these amenities has resulted in a rapid and welcomed rise in tourism.

The UAE is a founding member of the Gulf Cooperation Council

Currency is issued by the UAE Central Bank, which is located in Abu Dhabi. The paper notes that comprise this money are called dirhams, and each dirham is divided into 100 fils.

(GCC). Through this organization, the UAE works together with Saudi Arabia, Oman, Bahrain, Qatar, and Kuwait to increase economic cooperation among member nations. Through consultation and consensus, the GCC works to develop policies concerning banking, investment, and finance; telecommunications and intellectual property rights; and transportation as well as trade.

Hamad bin Mohammad al-Sharqui, emir of al-Fujairah, walks past an honor guard, accompanied by Venezuelan president Hugo Chavez (left). As one of the rulers of an emirate in the UAE, Hamad bin Mohammad is a member of the federation's Supreme Federal Council, a governmental body that establishes policy for the federation.

POLITICS IN THE UAE

Before the United Arab Emirates was established in 1971, each of the seven emirates already had its own government. The rulers of the emirates realized that to successfully govern the federation, they needed to decide exactly what powers would be allocated to the federation and list them in a provisional constitution. Any powers not listed in the constitution would remain under the control of individual emirates. This is similar to the constitution of the United States, wherein powers and rights not specifically granted to the federal government remain in the control of states and citizens.

The UAE's system of government is similar to that of the United States as well. For example, the federation has executive, legislative, and judicial branches. However, the executive branch dominates in the UAE without the checks and balances that are in place in the United States.

Governmental bodies include the Supreme Federal Council (SFC), sometimes called the Supreme Council of Rulers or the Supreme Council of the Union. The rulers of the seven emirates are members of this council, which meets four times each year and establishes general policy in the UAE. The SFC elects the president and the vice president of the UAE and appoints judges to the Supreme Court. Both the president and vice president serve five-year terms, but the terms are indefinitely renewable. Each member of the SFC has one vote, but the dominant emirates, Dubai and Abu Dhabi, have the power to veto votes on really important matters.

The president appoints a Council of Ministers, which acts as a federal cabinet. This body is under the leadership of the prime minister (who is also the vice president of the federation). The Council of Ministers is the main source of legislative authority and, as such, it has the power to enact laws. These laws must then be **ratified** by the SFC.

There is another legislative body, called the Federal National Council (FNC) or National Assembly, that operates in an advisory capacity. The FNC is composed of 40 members who are appointed by the president. Members come from all of the emirates, but the larger, wealthier emirates hold more seats on the FNC. Members serve for two-year terms, but their terms can be renewed indefinitely. The main purpose of the FNC is to provide a forum for the discussion of important issues of national concern.

The UAE has an independent judiciary. The highest court is called the Federal Supreme Court, and it is composed of five judges. In addition to the Federal Supreme Court, there are lower-level Courts of First Instance that have the ***jurisdiction*** to hear cases. The legal system in the UAE incorporates many elements from the West, particularly in areas of commercial law, but it also has courts based on *Sharia* (Islamic law). Under the supervision of each ruler, cases in individual emirates are often decided by local custom.

The preliminary constitution of the UAE remained in effect from 1971 until it was made permanent in 1996. While there has been some discussion about moving toward a more democratic system of government, no actual steps have been taken toward that end. Unlike the United States, there are no political parties, and citizens are not permitted to vote for their leaders. While significant developmental changes have taken place in the UAE over the last several decades, the political system retains its strong tribal heritage. Political power remains hereditary, and the rulers of each emirate are members of the dominant tribe.

Combining tribal systems with modern politics has been key to the successful establishment and operation of the United Arab Emirates and the development of its distinct national identity. The best traditions of its tribal Bedouin past have been preserved and adapted while at the same time the government has been able to create a modern administration.

The colors used in the flag of the United Arab Emirates—red, green, white, and black—are also used in the flags of several other Arab countries. These colors were included in a 13th-century poem, which described the green Arab lands defended in black battles by the blood-red swords of Arabs whose deeds are pure white.

LOCAL GOVERNMENT

The local governments operating in each of the seven emirates have grown significantly over the last 30 years, yet there is much variety from one emirate to another. The constitution of the UAE reserves significant powers and substantial autonomy for the individual emirates. Each emirate retains control over **revenue** and mineral rights, for example, although a specified percentage of revenue from each emirate is transferred to the central budget of the UAE. Various factors—including the size of the emirate along with the population, wealth, and rate of development—affect the complexity of individual governments. The positions held on a federal level by members of the individual emirates are indicative of each emirate's financial and political influence.

A similarity among local governments is that each maintains a number of departments that manage areas such as finance, customs, and public works.

People living in remote settlements are sometimes served by a *wali*, or governor, appointed by the ruler. The *wali*'s job is to bring the concerns of citizens to the attention of the appropriate governmental department or individual. The ruler usually chooses a person who is already a leader among his fellow tribesmen for this honored position.

Through the government, many benefits, including better educational opportunities and vocational training, have come to people living in the smaller emirates. As a result, the populations of the emirates are better trained to work in various positions, and jobs that had once been handled by the federal government can now be taken over by locals. There are certain areas, however, where local authorities have been gradually and voluntarily relinquishing control to the federal government. The judiciary is one such example.

In addition to being the president of the United Arab Emirates, Sheikh Zayid is the ruler of the emirate of Abu Dhabi. In 1970 he established the National Consultative Council. Leaders from each of the major families and tribes in Abu Dhabi were invited to participate. This group is similar to the Federal National Council that was created a year later. Consultation and discussion are respected traditions in the UAE, and members of these councils are invited to express their opinions in a free and open manner without fear of reprisal. The creation of these councils represents the formalization of a traditional process into the official government.

TRADITIONAL GOVERNMENT

The leader of a tribe is called a sheikh. A sheikh is able to maintain his authority by keeping the support and loyalty of tribal members. The leader of the most powerful tribe living in an emirate most often becomes the ruler. This ruler is determined by **dynasty** and consensus of tribal members. The most powerful tribe is not always that tribe with the largest population. Power can be determined by other means.

An important custom is based on the belief that tribal members deserve to be heard by the ruler. Toward that end, sheikhs often hold a council, or *majlis*, during which members of the tribe can feel free to share their opinions and make requests of the sheikh. This custom has been at the center of traditional government for generations, and all citizens are welcome to attend these special councils. Requests made at a *majlis* may run the gamut from land requests to scholarship funds to business concerns. This is not a democratic assembly, and no votes are taken regarding matters under discussion or requests made. The sheikh makes the decisions; his rulings are final and there are no appeals.

In small emirates, the council being conducted by the ruler of the emirate remains the focus of attention for the population. Tribesmen may prefer to wait several days for the chance to speak directly to the ruler rather than taking their request to other government personnel. The ruler of al-Fujairah conducts a *majlis* at least once a week. Expatriates are invited to attend along with citizens. During Ramadan, the schedule of *majlis* in al-Fujairah is increased to every day. Councils like these demonstrate that traditional methods of government maintain their relevance and continue to play a vital role in the lives of the people of the UAE.

RELIGION

The vast majority of people in the Middle East are devout Muslims. Most followers of Islam are born into the religion, but one can become Muslim simply by reciting the profession of faith (*shahadah*)—"There is no god but Allah, and Muhammad is His prophet."

There are some similarities to Islam and the two monotheistic religions that preceded it, Judaism and Christianity. Muslims hold Moses and the

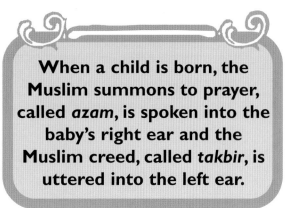

When a child is born, the Muslim summons to prayer, called *azam*, is spoken into the baby's right ear and the Muslim creed, called *takbir*, is uttered into the left ear.

Hebrew prophets in high regard. They also have a great deal of respect for Jesus, but consider him to be a prophet rather than the son of God. However, Muslims believe that the last and greatest of the prophets was Muhammad.

The central teaching of Islam is that there is one **omniscient** god. This is Allah, who created the universe, and man must surrender to His will. In fact, the word "Islam" is derived from the Arabic verb *aslama,* which means "surrender" or "submission." An individual who follows the teachings of Islam is called a Muslim, and the word Muslim means "one who surrenders to Allah." Statues and icons are forbidden in the Islamic religion, but some people carry small copies of the Qur'an with them at all times.

Muslims follow five basic teachings, or pillars, of the faith. The first is the *shahadah,* or profession of faith. Second is *salat,* a requirement to pray five times a day. Third is *zakat,* a commandment to share with those who are less fortunate. Fourth, *sawm,* is the tradition of fasting from dawn to dusk during Ramadan, the ninth month of the Islamic calendar. Finally, all adult Muslims who are able must make a special pilgrimage to Mecca and other holy sites (*hajj*) once during their lifetime.

Although there are a great variety of Muslim sects, there are two major divisions in the faith. Most Muslims—about 85 percent of the worldwide population—follow Sunni Islam. People who practice Sunni believe that they follow the true teachings of Muhammad. Within the Sunni division is the strict, conservative Wahhabi sect of Islam, which is followed by many Muslims in the UAE.

The United Arab Emirates is also home to a small community of Muslims who follow Shia Islam,

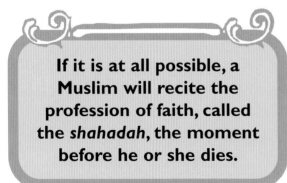

If it is at all possible, a Muslim will recite the profession of faith, called the *shahadah*, the moment before he or she dies.

Hundreds of thousands of Muslims pray before the Ka'aba, which is located in the Great Mosque at Mecca. Muslims—and the polytheistic Arab religions that preceded Islam—consider the Ka'aba to be the center of the earth, and the most sacred place of worship. In Arabic *Ka'aba* means "square" or "four sides," and the stone's sides are said to represent the four directions: north, east, south, and west.

the minority branch of the faith. Shiites make up less than 15 percent of the worldwide Islamic population, although some Middle Eastern states, like Iran, Bahrain, Iraq, and Lebanon, have Shiite majorities. In the UAE, about 16 percent of the population follows Shia Islam.

One cannot overemphasize the importance of Islam in the daily life of citizens of the UAE, where 96 percent of the population is Muslim. The tenets of Islam are strictly observed in the UAE. One can easily see it represented in food, dress, daily prayer, and law.

Muslims are called to prayer five times each day (at dawn, at noon, in the afternoon, at sunset, and at nightfall), but Friday, called *Yawm al-Jum'a* (the Day of Assembly), is a day of obligatory congregational prayer. Male Muslims are required to participate in Friday prayer as a group. For women, group prayer is optional. Muslims observe daily prayers faithfully whether they are alone in the desert or amid thousands in the city.

Worshipers in cities frequent Muslim places of worship called mosques. Some mosques are very large. The New Bazaar Mosque in Dubai, for example, can accommodate thousands of the faithful. The exterior of this mosque offers a festive atmosphere where one can purchase prayer beads and beautifully bound copies of the Qur'an.

While Muslims consider some parts of the Bible to be an important part of their own history, the Qur'an is the holy book of Islam. The 114 *surras* (chapters) in the Qur'an contain the tenets of the faith that Muslims live by every day.

It is ironic that the same religion that unites the people of the Middle East also divides them. The differences in religious belief between the Sunni and Shiite sects often create prejudice and carry over into many aspects of life. Disagreements between nations can take on a religious fervor. Enemies become infidels to be destroyed. Unfortunately, like other religions that profess to have been divinely revealed, there are followers of Islam who interpret its scripture in a manner that justifies intolerance and harsh dogma. While mosques do have imams (leaders of the congregation), there currently is no hierarchy for leadership of the religion as a whole. This leaves the words and teachings of the Qur'an open to interpretation by anyone.

The term *jihad* has become familiar to individuals all over the world. The word is used to describe a struggle against enemies of God. It is generally believed that this refers to a struggle within each individual. Some extreme Islamic **fundamentalists** have interpreted the term to mean a holy war, specifically a holy war against western governments and societies. Other people argue this is a perversion of the true teachings of Islam. According to them, intolerance, harsh dogma, and extremism are in direct contrast to Islamic teachings. One of the leaders of the World Conference on Religion and Peace has stated that "Respecting the sanctity of life is the cornerstone of the religion," and that "Peace is the essence of Islam."

Islam enters into all phases of life and law in the UAE, and its importance as the ultimate source of legislation has been made part of the constitution.

Arab men hold their *jambiyas* (long, slightly curved daggers) aloft during a procession in Dubai. Although approximately 2.5 million people live in the United Arab Emirates, fewer than 900,000 hold full citizenship.

The People

The culture of much of the Arab world is reflected in the population of the United Arab Emirates. For the most part, the people share the same religion and language. They are the descendents of a hardy people who were able to survive the harsh conditions of desert life or plunge into the depths of the sea to harvest pearls. In general the descendants of nomads and seafaring warriors living in the United Arab Emirates today can be described as warm, welcoming, and generous. They have proven themselves to be resilient and adaptable to the rapid changes that have taken place in their land.

The availability of jobs has attracted many foreign laborers. Today, **expatriates** account for more than 90 percent of the workforce in the UAE. They are employed in every sector of the economy with the notable exception of government positions. Citizens of the UAE usually occupy these jobs.

Foreign workers and their families now account for more than two-thirds of the country's total population.

There is a preference for large families in the UAE, and the government encourages its citizens to have many children. That, combined with improvements in medical care and the many young foreign workers, means the population of the UAE is relatively young.

Asians—including people from Pakistan, Bangladesh, Sri Lanka, India, and the Philippines—represent approximately two-thirds of the non-native population. Most of the remaining non-native residents come from Jordan, Egypt, Palestine, Yemen, Oman, and Iran. There are also many people from Europe and the West living in the UAE.

The official language of the United Arab Emirates is Arabic, although English, Urdu, Hindi, and Persian are also spoken.

EDUCATION AND SOCIAL WELFARE

The UAE now allocates 10 percent of its annual budget to education. Primary education between the ages of 6 and 12 is mandatory, and both primary and secondary education are free to all citizens of the UAE. Women are encouraged to take advantage of educational opportunities and to later enter the workforce.

The adult **literacy** rate is estimated at about 80 percent. This is among the highest rates in the Arab world, and represents an impressive increase since the formation of the federation, when the literacy rate was less than 50 percent.

In 1977, UAE University opened its doors in Al Ain with 519 students. By the middle of the 1990s that number had grown to approximately 12,000, with three-fourths of the students being women. Two men's colleges of technology opened in 1988, and two more have since opened for women.

Abu Dhabi boasts a Cultural Foundation that acts as a national center where individuals attend cultural events, take classes,

Most of the approximately 2.5 million people living in the UAE can be found along the coast. Al Ain, along the eastern border with Oman, is also a population center.

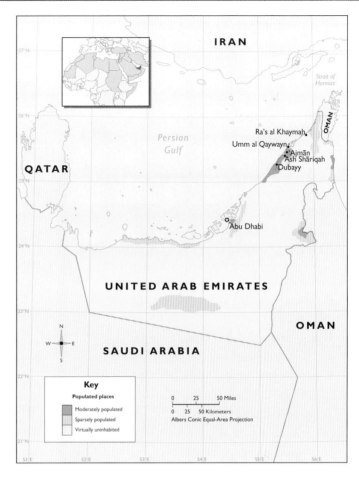

have access to historical documents, and conduct research. Classes offered to citizens include painting and sculpture, computer literacy, Arabic calligraphy, music, and memorization and recitation of the Qur'an. The Cultural Foundation also conducts an annual festival for children.

There is very little poverty in the UAE, although disparities in the standard of living do exist between emirates. A large part of Abu Dhabi's wealth is devoted to the welfare of people living in the poorer emirates. Health care is government financed and has improved greatly since the federation was formed. The infant mortality rate has been drastically reduced, and average life expectancy is now about age 74. There is little crime, and tolerance is evidenced by the fact that all emirates allow expatriates to participate in their own religious and cultural organizations and practices.

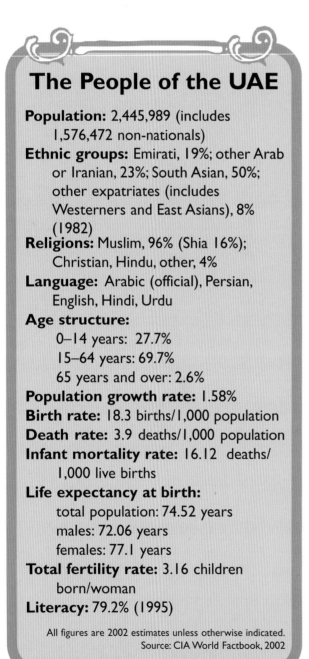

The People of the UAE

Population: 2,445,989 (includes 1,576,472 non-nationals)

Ethnic groups: Emirati, 19%; other Arab or Iranian, 23%; South Asian, 50%; other expatriates (includes Westerners and East Asians), 8% (1982)

Religions: Muslim, 96% (Shia 16%); Christian, Hindu, other, 4%

Language: Arabic (official), Persian, English, Hindi, Urdu

Age structure:
  0–14 years: 27.7%
  15–64 years: 69.7%
  65 years and over: 2.6%

Population growth rate: 1.58%

Birth rate: 18.3 births/1,000 population

Death rate: 3.9 deaths/1,000 population

Infant mortality rate: 16.12 deaths/ 1,000 live births

Life expectancy at birth:
  total population: 74.52 years
  males: 72.06 years
  females: 77.1 years

Total fertility rate: 3.16 children born/woman

Literacy: 79.2% (1995)

All figures are 2002 estimates unless otherwise indicated.
Source: CIA World Factbook, 2002

FAMILY LIFE

Traditional and modern elements blend beautifully in the society and culture of the UAE. In Islam, the family is considered to be a gift from God. The basic social structure is stable and conservative thanks to the traditions of Islam and the heritage of a tribal society.

Both indigenous and western dress can be seen on the street reflecting a blend of traditional and modern influences. Most male members of the UAE wear the traditional *dishdasha*, a loose-fitting white garment that is comfortable in hot weather. The traditional garb for women is more confining, as most women still wear the *abayah*, a black garment that envelops the body, and the *burka*, a black veil or facemask. However, some young, educated women are starting to abandon this traditional dress in favor of more comfortable attire.

The government subsidizes

A fountain projects water into the air at the Abu Dhabi cultural center. The center is a place where residents of the UAE can learn more about their past.

housing, and modern air-conditioned units are available to most of the urban population. Some families live in houses while others live in apartments. People who inhabit rural areas often live in more traditional housing. Some of the remaining nomadic Bedouin continue to use tents.

Most people in the Middle East place family above all other things. The positions of individuals within the family are determined by traditions, and obligations and loyalty to family are paramount.

As in other Arab countries, the society of the UAE is patriarchal. Important family decisions are made by the father, and he is also the primary wage earner.

Children are showered with love, but behavior that is rebellious is not tolerated. Children are expected to conform to strict rules regarding dress and behavior and to always treat elders with respect. The honor of the family is placed in extremely high regard. Individuals are judged by the behavioral standards of the society throughout their lives, and actions that are considered to be improper can threaten the honor of the family. Individuals are taught at an early age to feel shame regarding unaccepted behavior and that it is their duty to protect the honor of the family.

Traditionally, families serve food on dishes placed on a carpeted floor, and people sit on the floor while eating. Most people eat a light breakfast often consisting of dates and coffee, but sometimes a type of pasta is included. Lunch is a large meal, which almost always includes a main dish of meat or fish with rice. Some popular side dishes include *tabbouleh*, *hummus*, and stuffed grape leaves. Flat bread is also usually served. Dinner is a more modest meal.

Several customs surround the drinking of *ghawah* (coffee), which is served at both the beginning

The UAE is a patriarchal society and the names of both male and female children reflect the father's side of the family. The father's first name is used as the middle name of both boys and girls, and the father's family name is used as their last name. The family name is main source of a person's identity, and women keep their father's family name rather than taking their husband's last name after marriage. Sometimes the word *bin*, meaning "son of," is included in a man's name and *bint*, meaning "daughter of," is included in a woman's name.

and the end of the meal. Although it is unsweetened, coffee is often flavored with cardamom or cloves. The small cups used for coffee do not have handles. They are always filled just halfway and although more may be offered, it is impolite to drink more than three cups. When the third cup is empty, guests extend the cup in front of them and tilt it from side to side. This is a signal that the person is finished and the cup can be removed. This ritual also signifies that the meal is over. Dessert is usually served with coffee at the end of lunch. While conversation can take place for an extended period of time before a meal, it is not engaged in after the meal has been completed.

THE ROLE OF WOMEN

Female children are taught from an early age to adopt modest dress and behavior, as is specified in the Qur'an. To many Muslims, this means that only the hands and feet of a woman can be exposed in

A variety of appetizers that might be served at a meal in the United Arab Emirates, including flatbreads, hummus, peppers, and various peas, beans, and legumes.

Three female police officers pose for a photograph in 1999. In that year, 20 women were permitted to join the police force in the emirate of Ajman. Women have more freedom in the UAE than in countries such as Saudi Arabia, although Islamic custom dictates that headscarves be part of these officers' uniforms.

public. Historically, this was the case in the UAE. While young girls from wealthy families could be seen in public wearing bright clothes and gold jewelry, as they approached puberty girls would disappear behind the traditional garments that covered them from head to foot. Colorful attire and jewels were often worn beneath street attire, however, and women could show them when visiting female friends.

For most of the older women living in the UAE, the center of life and daily activity remains the family. Since the federation was formed new opportunities have opened up for women, and they now comprise approximately 15 percent of the work force. Although girls and boys still attend separate schools, 98 percent of all girls and young women who are eligible to attend school now do so. In fact, females outnumber males in attendance at every grade level. Women also hold more teaching positions than men, and more of them work in the field of health services. Positions in the government continue to open up for women, and they currently occupy 40 percent of all government jobs. Although women are not allowed to serve in combat, they can hold positions in the military, and the first female pilot in the UAE recently graduated from Dubai Aviation College.

The Women's Federation of the UAE is credited with most of the improvements that have been made in women's lives. Composed of six major groups with a total of 31 branches, this hardworking organization has been serving women in every emirate since its inception in 1975. The powerful group has the authority to conduct discussions and enter into agreements with governmental departments and ministries. It operates under an independent charter and can make suggestions for amendments and even new laws concerning women and their interests.

CULTURE AND ACTIVITIES

Each year there are several events that celebrate the diversity and richness of the culture of the UAE. Islamic holidays are important to the entire country. Each emirate operates its own libraries and museums. The Center for Documentation and Research, located at the Abu Dhabi Cultural Foundation, is a national archive. Research on the history of the UAE is stored here and is available to scholars from around the world. Sharjah is home to a fine arts museum and a theater.

All aspects of cultural traditions, including dance and music, are important to the people of the UAE. National holidays and family weddings are just two of the occasions where native songs and dances are performed, although traditionally, men and women

A falconer practices his sport in the desert near Al Ain.

dance separately from each other. The *na'ashat* is a dance performed by women. During the dance each woman places her right hand on her chest and then sways from side to side. Men often perform the *ayyala*, during which they hold swords or sticks. Drums beat rhythmically while rows of men holding these implements move back and forth toward and away from each other simulating battle. Common musical instruments include the *nai* (an Arabian flute), drums in several shapes and sizes, and the *rababa* (an instrument with strings).

Several sports that are thought of as western are gaining a following in the UAE. Golf, auto racing, and soccer have all become popular. At the same time, many traditional activities of the Arabian Gulf maintain their popularity, including falconry and the racing of Arabian horses. Interest in horse racing in particular has grown, and the Dubai World Cup is now the richest horse race in the world as it offers a multimillion-dollar prize. Camel racing is also a popular sport in the United Arab Emirates.

The view across the Dubai Creek shows the skyline of Dubai, while a small boat ferries passengers across the creek. Dubai is the UAE's second-largest emirate, with a population of nearly 900,000.

Communities

Each of the seven individual emirates that comprise the United Arab Emirates—Abu Dhabi, Dubai, Sharjah, Ajman, Umm al-Qaiwain, Ras al-Khaimah, and al-Fujairah— has a distinct community and a personality all its own.

ABU DHABI

Occupying 26,000 square miles (67,314 square kilometers), Abu Dhabi is the largest of the emirates and is also home to the largest population. It is ruled by Sheikh Zayid bin Sultan al-Nahyan, who is also the president of the entire federation. The coastline of Abu Dhabi was once considered among the best in the world for the collection of pearls, but that industry declined in the 1930s.

In 1962, Abu Dhabi began to export oil from the offshore field of Umm Shaif. Oil sales revived the economy and led to changes in every aspect of life. Today, Abu Dhabi is the major oil producer in the UAE, producing approximately 85 percent of the annual yield.

The emirate of Abu Dhabi is home to the city of the same name. In 1971 Abu Dhabi was little more than a few hundred shacks made of mud and a mud fort. Today, the city is a bustling urban center inhabited by almost a million people. The city of Abu Dhabi houses the center of business life and government in the United Arab Emirates. Embassies from around the world and headquarters of international oil companies are located here. Tall, sophisticated buildings; luxury hotels; modern shopping malls; and state-of-the-art computer and communication systems can all be found in Abu Dhabi. Impressive parks and gardens are available to the public, and green belts line city streets.

This capital city organizes festivals for the benefit of residents and tourists throughout the year. One example is the Abu Dhabi Shopping Festival. Held each March, it offers great bargains and prizes at all of the shopping malls along with street entertainers and incredible fireworks displays.

DUBAI

At 1,000 square miles (2,589 square kilometers), Dubai is the second-largest emirate. It is a significant producer of oil and a prosperous trading center. Forty-nine airlines provide service to the emirate. Sheikh Maktoum bin Rashid al-Maktoum is the ruler of Dubai and is also the vice president and prime minister of the UAE federation. The famous Dubai Creek provides a natural harbor and also divides Dubai city (population 860,000) into two parts. Wooden boats serve as water taxis on the Creek, but bridges, a tunnel, and taxicabs also shuttle people from one side of the water to the other.

In the 1940s the ruler of Dubai persuaded the British to use Dubai as their main port when traveling between Britain and India. This strategic location on the Arabian Peninsula established the

Men pray in the street near a mosque in Dubai.

city of Dubai as one of the most important trading centers in the world. The dry docks in Dubai can repair the largest ships afloat. Dubai, sometimes called "the City of Merchants," is considered to be the commercial center of the UAE.

Like Abu Dhabi, Dubai has an annual Shopping Festival that is a major attraction for tourists. This is due at least in part to the fact that shopping is duty-free, but it is also a result of the exciting sporting events and entertainment that are offered during the festival. The goal of Dubai Summer Surprises, another festival, is to increase tourism during the summer months. As part of this festival, many entertaining programs are conducted daily at major shopping malls from July through mid-September.

SHARJAH

Sharjah is located between Dubai and Ras al-Khaimah, interrupted by the small Omani enclave of Ajman. It is ruled by Sheikh

Sultan bin Muhammad al-Qasimi, a descendant of the seafaring Qawasim tribe. In 1987, the older brother of Sheikh Sultan tried to take over control of the emirate but failed in his attempt. The brother then became the deputy ruler.

This emirate has a population of approximately 400,440 people and is connected to the other emirates by a series of highways. The coastline is about 19 miles (30 km) long. The city of Sharjah is the third largest in the UAE, and the port at the Sharjah Container Terminal was the first in the Middle East to have fully equipped container facilities. Another port, at Khorfakkan, offers important facilities to ships that are in the area but do not wish to enter the Arabian Gulf. Sharjah also has the distinction of having been the

A fish market in Sharjah, the fourth-largest emirate in the UAE.

site of the first school in the United Arab Emirates. It opened its doors in 1953. Most of the oil produced annually in the UAE that does not come from either Abu Dhabi or Dubai comes from this emirate.

Saudi Arabia donated a large amount of money to help pay for construction of the King Faisal Mosque in Sharjah. In exchange, this emirate agreed to make consumption of alcohol illegal. The impressive King Faisal Mosque can hold 3,000 worshipers at one time.

Although it is not famous for festivals, Sharjah is the capital for the sport of cricket in the UAE. In fact, people who follow this sport across the world have come to regard Sarjah highly for its one-day cricket internationals. Sharjah is also well known for its camel races. In addition, the emirate has museums that specialize in art, science, culture, archaeology, and Islamic history.

RAS AL-KHAIMAH

Ras al-Khaimah has the distinction of being the northernmost emirate in the UAE. Sheikh Saqr bin Muhammad al-Qasimi is the ruler of this land of approximately 928,360 people. Archaeological excavations have uncovered historical evidence in Ras al-Khaimah of an advanced civilization that conducted trade with people living in the area that is now India. Later historical records indicate that the city of Ras al-Khaimah once belonged to early Muslim caliphs. At that time the city was called Julfar. The city was also once a center of naval strength and was invaded by several groups of people, namely the Persians, the Portuguese, and the Dutch. Later, in the 18th century, it became al-Qawasim state.

Waters off the coast of Ras al-Khaimah are rich with tuna. Milk, poultry, fruits, and vegetables travel to the other emirates from Ras al-Khaimah. Mountains located in this emirate have made it possible to operate stone quarries and a cement factory. In addition to income received from these industries, the oilfield of Saleh brings revenue to the emirate's economy.

AJMAN, UMM AL-QAIWAIN, AND AL-FUJAIRAH

Ajman has a population of approximately 118,800 and is ruled by Sheikh Humaid bin Rashid al-Nuaimi. This small emirate encompasses just 259 square miles (100 sq km). The city of Ajman is situated on the Arabian Gulf coast and extends for 10 miles (16 km) between the emirates of Sharjah and Umm al-Qaiwain.

Sheikh Rashid bin Ahmad al-Mu'alla is the ruler of the Umm al-Qaiwain emirate located on the west coast of the UAE. Situated between Ajman and Ras al-Khaimah, this emirate is the home of approximately 35,150 people. Fishing and the cultivation of dates have provided the traditional occupations in the area. Seneyah Island is part of this emirate. This island has been declared a natural reserve for al-Qaram trees, deer, and birds. Long, pristine beaches and an enclosed lagoon are Umm al-Qaiwain's major tourist attractions. Officials hope to attract an increased number of tourists with "Dreamland," the world's largest aqua park.

The population of al-Fujairah is approximately 144,430, and the emirate is ruled by Sheikh Hamad bin Mohammad al-Sharqui. One distinction of the emirate is that it has one of the largest offshore **anchorages** for idle oil carriers, which are located in the Gulf of Oman. This gulf is much deeper and colder that the Arabian Gulf.

Historically, people made their living by fishing and farming. Today tourists are attracted to the clean beaches. Swimming, surfing, yachting, and deep-sea fishing are all popular activities.

FESTIVALS AND CELEBRATIONS

Muslims celebrate several religious holidays, and one celebrated all over the world is the prophet Muhammad's birthday (Meelad al-

Nabi). In the UAE, people come together to tell stories about Muhammad's life, his character, and his teachings.

During Ramadan, the ninth month of the Islamic calendar, adult Muslims are required to fast from sunup to sundown. Worship and acts of charity are also important aspects of Ramadan. After the sun goes down, family members gather for a big meal.

Eid al-Fitr (the "feast of fast-breaking") is an important social event that marks the end of Ramadan. Eid al-Fitr lasts for three days beginning on the first day of Shawwal, the tenth month of the Islamic calendar. Cities and villages in the UAE take on a festive atmosphere as people dress in their finest clothing and meet in mosques or open areas to pray and visit.

Eid al-Adha (the "festival of the sacrifice") occurs during Dhul-Hijjah, the last month of the Islamic calendar. This is a time to remember the willingness of the patriarch Ibrahim (Abraham) to sacrifice his son Ishmael as Allah commanded. In the Muslim retelling of this event, when Allah recognized Ibrahim's willingness to obey His commands, he allowed Ibrahim to slaughter a sheep instead. Muslims around the world reenact this scene by ritually slaughtering sheep or other animals. The meat is carefully divided into thirds and distributed to the poor, to relatives and neighbors, and to the family. Eid al-Adha also marks the end of the *hajj* period, during which Muslims make their pilgrimage to Mecca.

Lailat al-Mi'raj (the "night of the journey") is a celebration of the ascension of Muhammad into paradise. According to tradition, Muslims observe this religious holiday by reciting special prayers and reading from the Qur'an during the evening.

Of the secular holidays that are observed in the United Arab Emirates, the most popular is the annual celebration of the formation of the UAE federation, National Day. Major cities in the emirates are decorated with lights, and there are civic displays of pride during this event, which takes place on December 2.

General Norman Schwarzkopf, commander of the international coalition that liberated Kuwait during the 1991 Gulf War, presents an award to Major General Muhammad Said al-Badi, chief of staff of the United Arab Emirates' armed forces, for his role in the conflict.

Foreign Relations

Unity among all Arab nations has been a consistent goal of the UAE. Several regional and international organizations have offices in the UAE, and the federation maintains active membership in many organizations, including the Arab League, the Organization of the Islamic Conference (OIC), and the United Nations. Additionally, the UAE is a member of the World Bank and the International Monetary Fund.

The UAE has established diplomatic relations with 143 countries, including Russia, Japan, the People's Republic of China, the United States, and much of Western Europe. By the end of 2001, there were 52 consulates in Dubai, 69 embassies in Abu Dhabi, and 35 nonresident ambassadors accredited to the UAE. The United Arab Emirates have two permanent missions to the United Nations (one in Geneva and the other in New York), 44 embassies, and seven consulates.

The emirates work together toward their mutual benefit,

Arab leaders participate in a meeting of the Gulf Cooperation Council.
Six Gulf states formed the GCC in 1981.

to promote harmony and to achieve protection for all. They have
been successful at achieving unity among the seven member emirates, and they apply the same ideology to foreign policy. They have
advocated a consistent policy of communication and consensus in
order to resolve disagreements and enhance cooperation in the
Arabian Gulf region and the broader Arab world.

One of the main goals of the UAE has been to develop and
strengthen ties to neighboring countries in the Arabian Peninsula.
Toward that end, the Gulf Cooperation Council (GCC) was formed
in 1981 at a summit conference in Abu Dhabi. The conflict between
Iran and Iraq that existed at the time was a **catalyst** for the formation of the organization. Member nations include the UAE, Saudi

Arabia, Kuwait, Qatar, Bahrain, and Oman. With the six member countries working together to ensure their security, the GCC has become an effective and widely respected organization. The invasion of Kuwait, a member of the GCC, in August 1990 represented a major challenge for the organization.

Since Saddam Hussein came to power in Iraq during the late 1970s, Iraq has been an aggressor nation that has tried to expand its territory into bordering countries. This has made its neighbors uncomfortable—the Gulf States do not want to get sucked into war with Iraq, or have to deal with the problem of refugees from war-torn countries.

In September 1980, Iraq invaded Iran, beginning a long and costly war. Disputes over national borders and interference with the internal affairs in the other country were among many factors that contributed to the eight-year-long Iran-Iraq War. The GCC nations attempted to remain neutral during the conflict, although the UAE worked with the United Nations to seek a resolution to the fighting. The armed conflict continued until August 1988 when both sides accepted a cease-fire arrangement sponsored by the United Nations. Each country suffered great losses as a result of the war, yet neither made any significant gains either politically or territorially.

In August 1990, Iraq invaded and occupied Kuwait, its tiny neighbor. One of the first Arab leaders to offer support to Kuwait was President Zayid of the United Arab Emirates, and the rest of the Arab world followed in condemning this act of aggression by Iraq's Saddam Hussein. Ultimately, at the urging of key Arab countries like Saudi Arabia and the UAE, the United States organized an international military coalition against Iraq. During the 1991 Gulf War, the forces of this 34-nation coalition drove Iraqi soldiers from Kuwait. The United Arab Emirates provided support for this international coalition, and armed forces from the UAE participated in

Sheikh Zayid bin Sultan Al Nahyan (right) meets with King Abdullah of Jordan in Abu Dhabi, to discuss bilateral ties. Since the formation of the UAE in 1971, Sheikh Zayid has attempted to maintain good relations with the other Arab nations.

the Gulf War. After the war ended with the liberation of Kuwait, the UAE was one of the first nations to offer financial assistance for rebuilding Kuwait.

After these conflicts, the United Nations imposed **sanctions** against Iraq. These sanctions, and the international condemnation of policies by the regime in power in Iraq, were supported by the United Arab Emirates. The sanctions have had serious consequences for the people of Iraq, however, and during the late 1990s the leaders of the UAE argued for the sanctions to be lifted. At the same time, the government of the United Arab Emirates provided generous humanitarian aid to the people of Iraq, while working to be certain that the financial aid ended up in the hands of the people it was intended for, rather than the rulers of Iraq.

THE UAE AND ITS NEIGHBORS

The Gulf War has not been the only time that the Arab nations of the region took sides against one another. On the Arabian Peninsula, some boundaries seem to shift as easily as sand in the desert, and territorial disputes have been common. Bahrain and Qatar, Iraq and Kuwait, and Saudi Arabia and Yemen have all been involved in border disputes. The UAE has worked to strengthen the League of Arab States and to improve relations between Arab countries. On the relationship between neighbors on the Arabian Peninsula, Sheikh Zayid said:

> Relations between the Arab leaders should be based on openness and frankness: They must make it clear to each other that each one of them needs the other, and they should understand that only through mutual support can they survive in times of need. A brother should tell his brother: you support me, and I will support you, when you are in the right. But not when you are in the wrong. If I am in the right, you should support and help me, and help to remove the results of any injustice that has been imposed on me.

Throughout the 1990s, Sheikh Zayid worked to convince leaders of the need for an Arab summit conference. The goal was to provide a forum for leaders of Arab countries to openly and honestly discuss their disputes. The first such conference took place in 2001 in Jordan. In addition, although open dialogue and cooperation are important, it is not always possible for all members of the Arab League to agree unanimously. Because of this, Sheikh Zayid became the first Arab leader to advocate a revision in the charter of the Arab League that would allow decisions to be made based on majority consensus.

The United Arab Emirates itself has not been exempt from territorial disputes. In the mid-1950s, religious fundamentalists from Saudi Arabia occupied villages around the Buraimi Oasis, which is located near the borders between Abu Dhabi, Oman, and Saudi Arabia. This became international news. With the aid of the British, soldiers from Oman and Abu Dhabi ultimately forced the Saudis to withdraw. This disagreement has never been formally settled. In 1972, an international boundary was drawn through

Iranian Foreign Minister Kamal Kharazi (right) meets with Sheikh Hamdan bin Zayid al-Nahyan, the UAE's minister of foreign affairs, to discuss the long-standing dispute between the Iran and the UAE over the islands of Abu Musá and the Greater and Lesser Tunbs.

the oasis, placing three communities in Oman and six in Abu Dhabi. None of the governments has taken steps to formally recognize the agreement, however.

In addition, there have been numerous disagreements with Oman over the boundary between the two countries. Each side has worked to settle their dispute without violence, and in 2000 they announced the ratification of a boundary agreement that resolved the most important issues. The **delimitation**, however, was not finalized. Nevertheless, the Oman-UAE Border Accord marked a significant step forward in relations between these neighbors on the Arabian Peninsula.

Iran and the United Arab Emirates have had an ongoing territorial dispute since the early 1970s. The dispute concerns ownership of the islands of Abu Musá and the Tunbs in the lower portion of the Arabian Gulf. The islands are of interest because of their strategic importance near the Strait of Hormuz, through which one-fifth of the world's oil passes. Also, it is believed there may be large amounts of oil under Abu Musá.

The island was claimed by the emirate of Sharjah, although in the late 1960s the ruler of Iran claimed that the islands had once belonged to that country. In 1971, the leaders of Sharjah and Iran negotiated an agreement under which neither side gave up its claim to sovereignty, but Iran was permitted to establish military bases on Abu Musá. Iran soon occupied the Greater and Lesser Tunbs as well—a move that angered the UAE and other Arab countries, but one which they were powerless to do anything about. During the Iran-Iraq War, the UAE submitted its claim on the islands to the United Nations. However, this was never resolved, and Iran ultimately forced all foreigners from the islands and took over total control in April 1992.

Palestinian students work on their lessons in their school in the Gaza Strip. The United Arab Emirates has given generously to help the Palestinians, and has supported their goal of independent statehood.

Discussions over the issue have been intense. Leaders in Iran have stated that the UAE would have to "cross a sea of blood" to recover these islands. Although the UAE has requested a diplomatic solution to the problem, it seems unlikely that Iran will relinquish control. The issue remains a sensitive one in the UAE.

Despite this, the United Arab Emirates have tried to maintain friendly relations with much-larger Iran. Even during the Iran-Iraq War, the lines of communication remained open despite the UAE's support of Iraq during the later years of the fighting. The UAE also attempted to mediate the conflict between the two major regional powers.

ISRAEL AND THE PALESTINIANS

Like most of the Arab states, the United Arab Emirates does not officially recognize the state of Israel. Since coming to power in the early 1970s, Sheikh Zayid has supported the cause of the Palestinian Arabs, who claim that the Israelis forced them from their land in 1948 and have used various measures to oppress Palestinians since then. The UAE has given millions of dollars in support of Palestinian organizations, and has proclaimed its belief that peace in the region can not come about without the establishment of an autonomous Palestinian state.

After 1993, when the Oslo Accords created the Palestinian Authority to oversee parts of the West Bank and Gaza, the UAE began providing a great amount of financial aid to the region. The money was used to build hospitals, schools, a network of roads, and houses, as well as to repair Christian and Muslim holy sites in Jerusalem.

The United Arab Emirates has been a consistent contributor to the United Nations Relief Works Agency (UNRWA) and has participated in programs conducted by other groups and multilateral agencies to support Palestinian development.

When the peace process broke down in the fall of 2000, and the Palestinians began their second *intifada* by attacking targets in Israel, the United Arab Emirates increased its support for the Palestinian Authority. The UAE even purchased a house in Washington, D.C., for the Palestinian Authority to use as a headquarters in the United States.

The UAE's hostile stance toward Israel has not wavered throughout its history. A few years after the federation became independent, Syria and Egypt attacked Israel in October 1973. The UAE supported their forces during this conflict, which became known as the Ramadan War in Arab states, and the Yom Kippur War elsewhere. After Egypt and Israel negotiated a peace treaty in September 1978, with the help of U.S. President Jimmy Carter, the UAE broke off diplomatic relations with Egypt, the largest of the Arab nations. Full ties were not reestablished until late in 1987.

In April 2002, the UAE joined 18 other Arab nations in restarting an economic boycott of Israel, which had been eased during the mid-1990s. Some store owners and consumers in the UAE have decided to boycott American-made products as well, in response to U.S. support for Israel.

THE UAE AND THE WEST

The United Arab Emirates is highly respected within the international community. It has gained this reputation in part because of Sheikh Zayid's efforts to promote discussion and consensus as a means for resolving international questions and disputes.

The UAE's ties with Western nations were strengthened during the 1991 Gulf War, when the UAE provided air bases and other support for the international coalition. A good relationship with the West has enabled the UAE to strengthen its military through the purchase of advanced technology and weapons, such as jet fighters and helicopters from the United States, Great Britain, and France.

U.S. troops watch as a helicopter lands in the Iraqi desert during Operation Desert Storm. The United Arab Emirates was one of more than 30 countries that participated in military operations against Iraq during the 1991 Gulf War. Since the end of the war, the UAE has remained an important ally of the United States, but the federation's leaders have also called for an end to UN sanctions against Iraq.

The U.S. has also provided training for a Hawk missile program.

Great Britain continues to have close ties with the United Arab Emirates. The basis of the well-trained army of the UAE was an elite force called the Trucial Oman Scouts, which was led and trained by British officers during the 1950s and 1960s. After the UAE became independent in 1971, the British turned control of the Trucial Oman Scouts over to the federation's rulers. Today, the headquarters for this 65,000-member army is located in Abu Dhabi. Most of the officers are citizens of the UAE, though many of the regular soldiers come from other Arab or East Asian countries.

The United States was one of the first countries to recognize the independence of the UAE, and a U.S. ambassador has resided in the country since 1974. The good relationship between the two countries extends both to business and government.

There have been tensions between the U.S. and the UAE, however. In 2000 the United Arab Emirates became one of the first Arab countries to violate United Nations' sanctions against Iraq, when it sent an airplane with medical personnel and humanitarian supplies to the country. The sanctions had been in place since the 1991 Gulf War. In December 2000 Sheikh Zayid said the UAE felt "deep pain and concern" about suffering in Iraq caused by the sanctions.

The September 11, 2001, terrorist attacks on the World Trade Center in New York City and the Pentagon in Washington, D.C., also cause some strain on the relationship. The UAE had been one of the few countries to officially recognize the Taliban government, which ruled Afghanistan from 1996 until the fall of 2001; the U.S. blamed the Taliban government for allowing terrorists to train openly in Afghanistan, and ultimately went to war to force the regime from power after the Taliban refused to hand over Osama bin Laden and other terrorist leaders. In addition, the United Arab Emirates was linked to the hijackers who carried out the September 11 attacks—two of the terrorists were from the UAE, ten had false papers that had been created in Dubai, and it was discovered that funding for the attacks had been routed through banks in the federation.

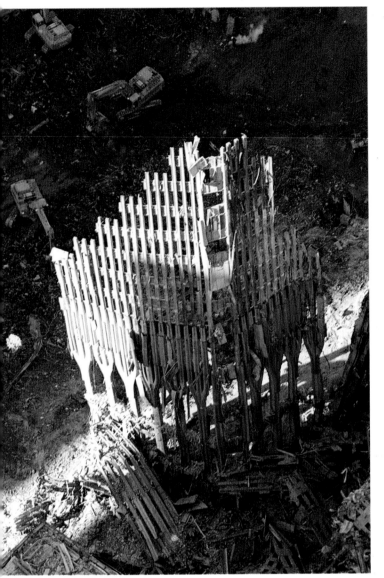

An aerial view shows the remains of the World Trade Center, which was destroyed by terrorists on September 11, 2001. After the attacks, the UAE's Sheikh Zayid said, "The UAE clearly and unequivocally condemns the criminal acts that took place last week in New York and Washington, resulting in the deaths and injuries of thousands. There should be a direct move and a strong international alliance to eradicate terrorism, and all those who provide assistance to it. . . . The UAE condemns all acts of terrorism everywhere."

When the United States announced its "war on terrorism," Sheikh Zayid and other leaders of the UAE renounced terror attacks. Banks in the UAE participated in U.S. efforts to freeze the accounts of organizations and individuals suspected of assisting al-Qaeda or other terrorist groups. As a result, the UAE is considered to be an important partner of the U.S. in its fight against terrorism.

Since 1973, the UAE has expended billions of dollars in foreign economic aid. Although most of this aid has gone to Arab or Islamic countries and causes, clearly the United Arab Emirates is concerned with stability around the world and has extended a helping hand to many nations.

CHRONOLOGY

2500 B.C.: The Umm an-Nar culture begins to develop in the region of the modern-day United Arab Emirates.

after 1200 B.C.: Camels are domesticated, and a primitive irrigation system is developed.

circa 600 B.C.: The Achaemenids, from Persia, control the UAE region.

circa A.D. 200: The Persian Sassanids take control of the UAE region.

632: The prophet Muhammad dies, but his new religion, Islam, continues to spread throughout the Arabian Peninsula.

1258: The Mongols capture Baghdad, ending the rule of the Abbasid caliphs.

1497: Vasco da Gama sets out from Portugal; he will sail around the southern tip of Africa, then north to India, establishing a Portuguese trade route. The Portuguese will soon send their navy to protect ships, and take over trade in the Arabian Gulf region.

1700s: Ras al-Khaimah and Sharjah begin to develop as strong states.

1820: British forces destroy the city of Ras al-Khaimah; coastal Arab sheikhs sign peace treaties with the British government, leading to the territorial name the Trucial States.

1853: The British promise to protect the Arabian Gulf area from attacks by other people.

1892: The sheikhs agree that they will deal with no other foreign governments without permission from the British.

1959: Oil is discovered in Abu Dhabi.

1966: Oil is discovered in Dubai.

1968: Britain says it will leave the Arabian Gulf region, and the sheikhs of the Trucial States begin to discuss forming a federation.

1971: The UAE is formed by Abu Dhabi, Dubai, Sharjah, Ajman, Umm al-Qaiwan, and al-Fujairah; Iran occupies the islands Greater Tunb, Lesser Tunb, and Abu Musá.

1972: Ras al-Khaimah joins the UAE.

1981: The UAE and other Arab countries form the Gulf Cooperative Council (GCC).

CHRONOLOGY

1991: The UAE joins the international coalition that fights in the Gulf War against Iraq; in July, the Bank of Credit and Commerce International (BCCI) collapses.

1996: Iran builds an airport on Abu Musá and a power station on Greater Tunb, reigniting the dispute over ownership of the islands.

1998: The UAE restores diplomatic relations with Iraq.

2000: The UAE pays nearly $8 billion for 80 fighter jets and missiles from a U.S. company.

2001: Sheikh Zayed bin Sultan Al Nahyan speaks out against the terrorist attacks on New York City and Washington, D.C., in September; the UAE freezes the bank assets of more than 60 organizations suspected of supporting terrorists.

2002: The UAE and other Arab countries restart an economic boycott against Israel.

2003: The United Arab Emirates signs a treaty with Oman delineating the borders of the two countries.

2004: Iran and the government of the UAE hold high-level meetings over the status of Abu Musa and the Greater and Lesser Tunb islands.

2005: UAE announces that partial parliamentary elections will be held for the first time. Half of the Federal National Council will be elected by the Emirates, while the other half will continue to be appointed.

anchorage—a place where vessels can be tied up or anchored offshore.

aquifer—an underground layer of water-permeable rock, sand, or gravel.

caliphs—the title of a Muslim ruler, which asserts religious as well as secular authority.

catalyst—something or someone that makes a change happen.

delimitation—to define the limits of.

dynasty—a powerful family or group that maintains its ruling position over a long period of time.

estuary—a water passage in which an ocean tide meets a river current.

expatriate—someone who leaves his or her native country to live elsewhere.

federation—a political unit formed from smaller units.

fundamentalist—a person who follows a strict interpretation of the doctrines of a religion.

gross domestic product—the total value of all goods and services produced within a country during a one-year period.

jurisdiction—the power, right, or authority to interpret and apply the law.

literacy—the ability to read and write.

masonry—the art of building or carving something out of stone or brick.

nomadic—relating to people who have no fixed residence, but move from place to place usually seasonally and within a well-defined territory.

omniscient—having infinite awareness, understanding, and insight.

plate tectonics—a theory in geology in which the lithosphere of the earth is divided into a small number of plates that float on the mantle.

potable—suitable for drinking.

racketeering—the act of engaging in a fraudulent scheme, enterprise, or activity.

ratify—to give formal approval to a treaty or agreement so that it becomes valid or operative.

revenue—money, income.

sanction—a coercive measure designed to force a nation violating international law to stop or yield to adjudication.

subsidy—a grant or gift of money, usually made by the government.

subsistence—relating to the means necessary to support life.

FURTHER READING

Cordesman, Anthony H. *Bahrain, Oman, Qatar, and the UAE: Challenges of Security.* Boulder, Colo.: Westview Press, 1997.

Crystal, Jill. *Oil and Politics in the Gulf.* Cambridge University Press, 1994.

Hiro, Dilip. *The Longest War: The Iran-Iraq Military Conflict.* New York: Routledge, 1991.

Hourani, Albert. *A History of the Arab Peoples.* Cambridge, Mass.: Belknap Press of the University of Harvard Press, 1991.

Hurriez, Sayyid Hamid Hamid. *Folklore and Folklife in the United Arab Emirates.* London: Curzon Press, 2001.

Ingham, Bruce. *Customs and Etiquette in Arabia and the Gulf States.* Kent, England: Global Books Ltd., 1994.

Kechichian, Joseph A., ed., *Iran, Iraq, and the Arab Gulf States.* New York: Palgrave, 2001.

Lewis, Bernard. *The Middle East: A Brief History of the Last 2,000 Years.* New York: Scribner, 1995.

McCoy, Lisa. *Qatar.* Philadelphia: Mason Crest Publishers, 2004.

Mehr, Farhang. *A Colonial Legacy: The Dispute over the Islands of Abu Musá, and the Greater and Lesser Tumbs.* New York: University Press of America, 1997.

Reich, Bernard and Gershon R. Kieval. *Israel: A Land of Tradition and Conflict.* Boulder, Colo.: Westview Press, 1993.

Ryan, Stephen. *The United Nations and International Politics.* New York: St. Martin's Press, 2000.

Shakir, M. H., trans. *The Qur'an.* Elmhurst, N.Y.: Tahrike Tarsile Quran, Inc., 1995.

Surrat, Robin, ed. *The Middle East, 9th ed.* Washington, D.C.: Congressional Quarterly Press, 2000.

Viorst, Milton. *Sandcastles: The Arabs in Search of the Modern World.* New York: Alfred Knopf, 1994.

Zahlan, Rosemarie Said. *The Making of the Modern Gulf States: Kuwait, Bahrain, Qatar, the United Arab Emirates, and Oman.* Garnet Publishing, Ltd., 1999.

http://www.cia.gov/cia/publications/factbook/geos/ba.html

The CIA World Fact Book provides handy facts regarding the UAE that can be viewed at a glance.

http://www.dubaicityguide.com

This Web site provides general information on the city of Dubai as well as day-to-day information regarding specific events.

http://www.uaeinteract.com/default.asp

This is the official Web site of the UAE and provides an absolute wealth of information on the country.

INDEX

Numbers in **bold italic** refer to captions.

INDEX

PICTURE CREDITS

CONTRIBUTORS

The **FOREIGN POLICY RESEARCH INSTITUTE (FPRI)** served as editorial consultants for the MODERN MIDDLE EAST NATIONS series. FPRI is one of the nation's oldest "think tanks." The Institute's Middle East Program focuses on Gulf security, monitors the Arab-Israeli peace process, and sponsors an annual conference for teachers on the Middle East, plus periodic briefings on key developments in the region.

Among the FPRI's trustees is a former Secretary of State and a former Secretary of the Navy (and among the FPRI's former trustees and interns, two current Undersecretaries of Defense), not to mention two university presidents emeritus, a foundation president, and several active or retired corporate CEOs.

The scholars of FPRI include a former aide to three U.S. Secretaries of State, a Pulitzer Prize–winning historian, a former president of Swarthmore College and a Bancroft Prize–winning historian, and two former staff members of the National Security Council. And the FPRI counts among its extended network of scholars—especially its Inter-University Study Groups—representatives of diverse disciplines, including political science, history, economics, law, management, religion, sociology, and psychology.

DR. HARVEY SICHERMAN is president and director of the Foreign Policy Research Institute in Philadelphia, Pennsylvania. He has extensive experience in writing, research, and analysis of U.S. foreign and national security policy, both in government and out. He served as Special Assistant to Secretary of State Alexander M. Haig Jr. and as a member of the Policy Planning Staff of Secretary of State James A. Baker III. Dr. Sicherman was also a consultant to Secretary of the Navy John F. Lehman Jr. (1982–1987) and Secretary of State George Shultz (1988).

A graduate of the University of Scranton (B.S., History, 1966), Dr. Sicherman earned his Ph.D. at the University of Pennsylvania (Political Science, 1971), where he received a Salvatori Fellowship. He is author or editor of numerous books and articles, including *America the Vulnerable: Our Military Problems and How to Fix Them* (FPRI, 2002) and *Palestinian Autonomy, Self-Government and Peace* (Westview Press, 1993). He edits *Peacefacts*, an FPRI bulletin that monitors the Arab-Israeli peace process.

LISA MCCOY is a freelance writer and editor living in Washington. She has had many articles published, and one of her short stories received an Honorable Mention award in L. Ron Hubbard's Writers of the Future contest. Her other works include *Qatar* and *Bahrain* in Mason Crest's MODERN MIDDLE EAST NATIONS series.